FOREWOR

I have talked about producing a picture book on Banwell for some years and it has become a bit of a joke with those that know me, as nobody, including myself, thought I would ever get started. What you see here is not what I intended but something I thought I could achieve in the time limit I set myself. It is a selfish book, composed for my own pleasure, but if readers find it of interest, it will make the project even more worthwhile.

The title may seem rather odd, but those who have lived in the village 50, 60, 70 years will know how the village has changed and even if the main cause of Banwell's problems, the heavy traffic, was taken away it is unlikely the shops and businesses would return.

The bombs in 1940 opened up Banwell's street scene. The local and county authorities as well as the Government then tried to open up a wide enough route through the village to make a bypass unnecessary during the 1960s and 1970s. This played into the hands of a few developers who took advantage of "restoring" or destroying more of our old street scene in the name of progress.

Banwell's bypass had been mooted as long ago as the 1920s, when my uncle Wally Richards helped the surveyor peg out the part of the proposed route before he left school in 1928. Why the planned bypass was never completed at this time I have been unable to find out and it is unlikely that the Second World War interfered with plans as this was some time away. During the 1950s and 1960s the idea of a bypass was unpopular because of the housing development that may have taken place between the bypass and the village to pay for the road itself.

We are now left with an authority that does not know what to do; the so-called road improvements that have been put in place only make matters worse. The village will go on suffering its traffic and the damage it does for the foreseeable future.

Fortunately, of late, Banwell has become home to people who have immersed themselves in village life, organising and helping to preserve events and traditions that would have disappeared completely without them. Sometimes we get a difference of opinion, but never enough to do lasting damage. During the same period an element has arrived that has not become an asset to village life, destroying what others try to achieve, abusing and commandeering that to which they have no right. Until the 1950s everyone knew what was village property and respected it; if you had not bought it, it was not yours.

During my researches I have heard and read of the many losses to the village, including the pond, the old West Street School and Malt house that could have given Banwell a Village Hall long before The Second World War. I have been involved in many public meetings over the years to save bits of the village, mostly without success as in the past. Two small triumphs, however, have resulted in saving Nos. 16-18 West Street from demolition, although the creating of the one way system has not helped here, and retaining the Old Fire Station, now about the last old village building to be used for public events other than the church.

This may sound as though I am fed up with Banwell but it is not so, I was born here and hope to die here, (but not just yet!). My mother's ancestors can be traced in

St Andrews Church records back to 1780 when James & Hester Horle came to Banwell. Our family have lived here ever since; we would not want, nor intend, to live anywhere else.

Please enjoy the book and look at Banwell as it was.

Roy Rice

Local Historian, whose other researches and writings include:The Bilbie family of Chew Stoke, Bellfounders & Clockmakers 1680-1830 and 18th & 19th Century Manual Fire Engines and their Makers.

❑ ❑ ❑ ❑ ❑ ❑ ❑

ISBN 978-1-901084-64-1

Banwell, Somerset

Pictures and notes of a village now lost

Roy Rice

Seldon's Boot & Shoe shop window prior to the demolition of the south side of East Street in 1965. The religious framed notice which says **"Watch and Pray"** was very apt for this building and the rest of Banwell. Also drawn in the dirty glass of the shop window was a German Swastika, appropriate, I thought, seeing the German bombers were the first ones to start the destruction of Banwell's street scene in 1940. (See J Day & Sons shop p.7).

Some of the photographs I have used may not be the best quality. I have used them for reasons I hope will become clear in the text; they could have been improved on the computer but that would have taken the production beyond my capabilities and my time limit.

I have tried to make what I have written as accurate as possible but would be happy to receive corrections. Being a bad researcher I have no references for much I have written and I hope I will be forgiven for this. Amongst the books I have used are, Search 1-23 Banwell Society of Archaeology Journal, Banwell Parish Council Minutes 1894-1971, George Bennett's History of Banwell, and Kellys Directories.

Index

Acknowledgements

As I have been collecting and copying photographs and information over many years I may not be able to remember all those who have helped me and the list below may be incomplete. So please forgive me if I have missed you. Those I remember are, Banwell Society of Archaeology collection, Stuart Angelinetta, John Baxter, David Bromwich, Barbara Buttimer, Brendon Cottrell, John Davis, Jen Diver, Maria Forbes, Mrs S Garner, Jane Gumm, Mrs Sue Gunn, Reg Harding, Bob & Jean Harris, Pat Hase, both the James Hunts, Ginnette Irving, Dave Lock, Derek Neads, Vergo Neate, Molly Nichols, Mrs Andrew Oliver, Fred Parker, William Parsons, Mrs Peters, David & Richard Pruen, June Rice, Martin & Lou Sheperd, Peter Shipton, Jim & Betty Tabrett, Mrs Pam Turner, Clive Wallace, Julie Willcox, Charlie Williams, Ciss, David & Tony Yarde, Anne Dawson, Pete Brownette, Derek and Maureen Newton.

Stan Croker for the album of unique Banwell photographs he let me buy from him, brother Wally for "kicking me", making suggestions and looking to see if it made "Banall" sense and the lady who wishes to remain anonymous, whose help is greatly appreciated..

Last but not least Nette (Rice) who dealt with all my requests for dates and names of families and buildings from the archives on Banwell she has researched over the years.

ISBN 1 901 084 64 7

East Street

The Square with loose chickens in front of Stephens' butchers shop whose food used to attract Ben the swan from the pond up Church Street through the back of The Bell to the Square for a feed. From a postcard dated 1905.

Looking along East Street in the late 1890's. The buildings on the right behind the butcher's shop were pulled down in 1967 and the butcher's shop itself about 1972 all, it was said, to ease traffic problems and provide a car park which was never to materialise.

The first property on the left of the last picture is the Bell Hotel; next door with the man on the wall, was Banwell's first Wesleyan Chapel built around 1792 on what is said to have been "Sally Fry's Bakery". In 1862 a new Chapel was built in West Street, so presumably the congregation moved there and this one changed into what was called the Literary Institute and was used as a sort of village hall where dances and meetings were held. Later the Institute, as we called it, became the workshop of F D Day Builders and Undertakers whose signboard can still be seen over their shop and house on the opposite side of the road. In the 1970's the Institute was turned into a private dwelling and renamed the Old Chapel, presumably the name "Institute" could give the wrong kind of impression of the building's uses.

Banwell's first Wesleyan Chapel in East Street known for many years as the Institute.

Here it is still the workshop of F D Day & Sons Undertakers & Builders.

The Gallery of the East Street Wesleyan Chapel, or the Institute, just before it was converted into a dwelling.

The South side of East Street before 1965. The function of the gazebo type building to the left of the picture is not known but was the sort of thing an artist would use as a studio. Albert Curl, known as "Rabbit", at one time had a paper and sweet shop here where he lived until 1948. On occasions Mr Curl would go into the Square with white gloves on and direct traffic and then leave when it got jammed

up. This side of the Gazebo was a butchers' shop next came James Day, 1906-1914, and his niece Ginny Slade and later Harry Nuttycombe in 1923. They all ran a livery stable with pony traps and over closed brake hire providing a regular service to Sandford Station and back. James Day's shop later became Seldon's Boot & Shoe shop, the sign that was over the door when the premises were pulled down. Next came Brafield's butchers shop that ran into the Square.

James Day's shop that was opposite the Vicarage entrance in East Street. Before this building became derelict in the 1960's it had been Seldon's Boot and Shoe shop. As mentioned before in this shop window just before the premises was demolished was a religious framed notice which said "Watch and Pray". James Day, the owner, is in the bowler hat.

South side of East Street, Genette's Hairdressers shop still open in 1962/3 amongst the derelict buildings

The north side of East Street not dissimilar from today, other that the centre cottage, which was renovated with no thought of matching in with the rest of the cottages.

South side of East Street from Towerhead end with Fire station doors immediate right. You can see how narrow it was and how the buses filled the road. To ease the traffic on holiday weekends, one policemen and two special constables would be on duty, one holding the traffic at Dark Lane, one holding the traffic at West Street by the Methodist Chapel, and one directing in the Square.

Banwell's New Merryweather Fire Engine the gift of Miss Fazakerley outside her home the Abbey on Saturday 19th December 1887. On this same day Miss Fazakerley also presented the Fire Station to the village.

East Street looking towards Towerhead. The Fire station on the left looking much the same as it does today. It was given in 1887 by Miss Fazakerley of the Abbey to house the new Merryweather Fire Engine she had also given to the village. See Search 16 by Rice Bros. The gentleman to the right with bowler hat and apron was Algie "Cutty" Stevens who had a butcher's shop and slaughterhouse where he stands. My grandmother said he was called "Cutty" as he stuttered and would repeat cut cut cut many times when asking the customer where to cut the meat. He shut his shop in 1916 because he did not agree with the wartime government telling him when and how he could sell his meat. The shop remained in a time warp kept in order by his niece until she died and the premises were sold in 1950. See Search 6 by C Cousins.

Banwell Abbey, Manor House, Court or Palace was one of the residences of the Bishops of Bath & Wells from the 13th century, except for a short period during the reformation, until the late 18th century when the Blackburrow's, a gentry farming family leased the Abbey estate. Around the 1870's Joseph Dyer-Sympson, who built Banwell Castle as a home in 1847, set about altering and rebuilding the Abbey to the building you see today. We have no record of the building in the time of the Bishops, I would like to think that Mr Dyer-Sympson tried to put the Abbey building back to what he thought it might have looked like in those early days, but unfortunately he died before completing the work.

Mr Edgington, a Banwell schoolmaster, managed to look around this building when it was empty and describes some of the interior in the Weston Gazette of 1880, including the Chapel in which marriages had taken place in the Bishops' time, but had been used as a cellar according to George Bennett during Blackburrow's time. Edgington wrote, "The walls are covered with

Banwell Abbey Chapel in the 1910's when the Murray family lived there.

life-sized figures representing former Abbots, Abbesses, and Bishops, in full ecclesiastical dress". "At the east is a stained glass window representing four young novices in the act of taking the veil. The centre light is occupied by the figure of the Bishop of Bath & Wells at that period, before him are standing two young novices in the act of receiving the imposition of his hands which will confine them within the walls of the Abbey for the rest of their lives. A side light is filled with the figure of the Lady Superior leading another novice to the Bishop to receive his pastoral benediction and their consecration to a monastic existence" Edgington also says this took place within the walls of the Abbey Chapel in August 1317, and goes on to describe the small west gallery fronted by twelve panels each with the names and arms of Bishops of Bath & Wells from William de Marchia 1293-1302 to John Still 1593-1608.

Edgington went on to describe the stained glass windows in the drawing room and "a handsome cornice bearing the name of Oliver King, Episcopus, 1496-1503". This cornice had been found under the floor when it was lowered to heighten the room.

In 1913 the Murray family owned the Abbey and on the 29th March that year Jean Wesson, Alison Tucker, Beatrice Lovell, and David Hill children of John Tucker and Mabel Wesson Murray were baptised in the Chapel of the Abbey. The Lord Bishop of the Diocese had licensed the Chapel for any service performed by the clergy of the parish.

The Chapel possibly survived until the Abbey was split in four in the 1950's when it was converted into a living room of what is now called "The Cloisters. Also see Banwell Abbey in Search 23 by David Bromwich.

1918 Banwell Fair

One of the few pictures of Banwell Fair, this one is dated 1918. The number of boys in this picture may reflect the date as most of the men would still be away in the war, or was it as Bill Keate told me, that it was cheaper for farmers to get boys rather than drovers to deliver their new bought stock. Bill relates a story that he and Albert Hodges took on to deliver a newly bought cow to Wick St Lawrence for a Mr Pimm; the delivery went well at first but for some reason across the moor the cow took flight and ran across the fields. Luckily Bill and Albert eventually caught the cow but by the time they got to Wick St Lawrence it was getting dark. Mr Pimm's housekeeper gave Bill & Albert a good feed and when Mr Pimm came in he must have been in a good mood for he gave them half a crown, one and thruppence each, which was a good sum in those days. Bill would have got into trouble when he got home so late that night, but his mother had the one and thruppence so Bill got away with it.

George Bennett in his historical notes on Banwell in the early 1800s tells of great numbers of fatted oxen brought to Banwell Fair and sold for victualling for the Navy in times of war.

Besides cattle being sold in Dark Lane, sheep along East Street and horses down Riverside (which meant you could not get through Banwell on Fair Day) there were sideshows and stalls in The Square with a rifle range and Pruett's small hand driven roundabout. The Pruett brother came from Congresbury and lost their lives in the First World War; after that their roundabouts were stored in a Congresbury field for many years until one Guy Fawkes Night someone thought they would make a good bonfire. Jesse Fletcher also remembers in Search 20 a large lady called Betsy Toms who sold fairings, sugar apples and balloons. She also remembers Mrs Foll of Hillside, now Cherrymead, on the corner of Dark Lane complaining of the mess from the cattle outside her gate. Mrs Foll still invited the auctioneers to lunch. The public houses on Fair Day also kept a couple of strong-armed men on the doors as the drovers and gypsies would fight one another.

Banwell Fair 1965, Derek Palmer selling cattle in Dark Lane.

A newspaper account written in Somerset dialect about 1922 talks of "What a Fair"; the writer says he'd seen more cattle on his employer's farm than at the fair this year, and he recounts the fairs he remembers in the past years with hundred of cattle, horses and sheep and all manner of other things being sold by two auctioneers.

About 1937 the fair was moved from East Street, Dark Lane and The Square to a portion of the Abbey Grounds on account of the increase in road traffic. When the fair came back to East Street and Dark Lane I do not know, but cattle and sheep were being sold there as late as 1965.

On Banwell Fair Day the Fire Station was always open and a roaring fire kept to ward off the January weather. We still have a roaring fire in the Fire Station on Banwell Fair Day but in the last few years we have found it difficult to have stalls along the side of the road in East Street owing to cars parking, but at least Banwell Fair continues albeit in a very limited form.

Sheep pens in East Street
at Banwell Fair 1965

Dr Anderson's car said to be the first in the village. The car is parked at the back of Eversleigh in East Street, the home of Dr Anderson; the driver is Jack Gardner who later ran a grocery shop in the Rhoddy.

❏ ❏ ❏ ❏ ❏ ❏ ❏

The Square, also known at one time as "Trafalgar" Square.

The Square in early-motorised days. Somewhere to the right of the cars in the bottom picture stood the Village Cross shown on George Bennett's map of 1812 which looked like the cross opposite the Ship & Castle public house in Congresbury. Bennett's map was copied from an earlier map of The Town of Banwell in 1770, by Richard Tuckey, which is now lost.

George Bennett says the cross was taken down and rebuilt in 1754 but was later thought to incommode (hinder) the passage of the streets and was pulled down about the year 1798. So you see Banwell has had a traffic problem for a long time. When the south side of East Street was pulled down in 1967 the butcher's shop was left until a new one was built further along East Street. This old shop survived until 1972 when it was demolished, and the "Square" as we knew it, disappeared as well. All this destruction and the traffic problems are still with us.

Brafield Butchers in The Square and East Street from the 1920's to the 1990's

West side of Banwell Square from a postcard dated 1909.

The preceding picture is the only one I have seen that shows not only the Coffee Tavern (left) and Thomas Hurley's (centre) but also the side of George Neate's shop going up the High Street. George Neate's shop occupied the garden area and more at the south side of The Ship and jutted out into the High Street.

The west side of Banwell Square, possibly on Banwell Fair day, seeing there are unsaddled horses and children about. The only thing wrong is that Dennis Day says in Search 18 that on fair days his father boarded up all the shopkeepers' windows to stop them being broken by the animals or those worse for drink – this did not appear to be the case this year.

In 1881 the Coffee Tavern or Coffee House behind was lived in by William Stephens shoemaker and it is listed as Coffee & Reading room. Bill Keate tells me there was also a billiard table there for the use of customers, perhaps to encourage them from the public houses.

A newspaper cutting of 1882 states, "Temperance sends us the following statement" and then goes on to list the improvements in the Coffee Tavern's takings under the new management. The new management, according to another cutting, were Mr & Mrs Webb who put on a well-received Supper with songs, recitations and games in February 1882. It must have taken some nerve to open a coffee shop so near to the two main public houses of the village with, I presume, the intent of trying to steal their customers. By 1901 Francis Tidball is listed at the Coffee Tavern, which later became better known as Tidball's Tearooms.

Continuing in The Square, we come to the shop of Tom Hurley, selling sweets and groceries. He was also a chimney sweep, umbrella maker, a Baptist and a staunch Liberal. I was told by the late Dennis Day that during the night his house was painted in the colours of the opposing political party, which made Mr Hurley see very red in the morning, and it just goes to show vandalism occurred in those days. Tom Hurley's daughter Edith, whom as I remember when I was a boy, married a Mr Smith and ran the shop until she died in 1948. The shop was taken over by Mr Semple, a grocer, and later by Mr Rider who ran a very successful V G Grocery shop there and expanded it into what was the old Coffee Tavern next door. Mr Rider later sold the shop to two young gentlemen that ran the business into the ground in a very short time and the shop closed.

According to a sermon read in the Methodist Chapel in 1921 the son of a Mr Treloar, who had a mat and basket shop where Tom Hurley lived, became "Lord Mayor of London". The 1851 census for Banwell gives John Treloar aged 46 Vendor in Coconut & Fibre Manufacturer Born at Almondsbury. One of his sons, William aged nine, was born at Winscombe in 1842.

I checked the internet and found that there was a William Treloar who was Lord Mayor of London and whose father had a coconut fibre and carpet business that his son took over to become Treloar's Carpet Co. This William was born in 1843, near enough, but at Southwark, London. These two Williams may be completely different people or was it that when William became Lord Mayor he wanted to disguise his humble beginnings in Banwell. Further research might reveal the truth! In Kelly's Directory for Banwell in 1861 a John Treloar is listed as Master of the Parochial School; this could be our William's father, either retired from his shop or being a school master as well, as the 1861 census still lists him as a shopkeeper.

The usual view of the third shop, George Neate's, adjoining what was the Ship Hotel as shown in many pre-First World War photographs, but never the side going up High street. The shop was run by George Neate and his wife and sold greengrocery, meal, corn, barley, maize, oats, other poultry mixtures

and also rabbits as you can see hung up on the side between the doors in one of the previous picture of the this shop (p.16). In one part of the shop Mrs Neate also ran a drapery business that must have conflicted with what her husband sold. This shop protruded out in to High Street and must have made it even worse to come out onto West Street than today. The shop was demolished just after the First World War, probably in 1921 after George Neate died. The garden on which the shop stood was reduced to its present size again to help Banwell traffic in the 1960's.

George Neate and his wife lived opposite this shop where his daughter Gertrude, who is probably the lady in the doorway of the shop across the road, later ran the grocer's and draper's here and much later just a sweet shop, which closed not long before her death in 1961. It later reopened as a gift shop, a hairdresser and was then converted into a private residence around the 1970's.

Meeting of the Hunt in Banwell Square from a postcard, dated 1910. Could this be one of the meets that, I believe, traditionally took place after Banwell Fair day?

❏ ❏ ❏ ❏ ❏

West Street

Top of West Street in 1893. The Ship Hotel on the left with its large stables. On the right behind the man in shirtsleeves is Butstone House, the offices of Willett's of Banwell Mill. Kelly's Directories between 1875 & 1889 list Thomas Willett as grocer, ironmonger, corn factor and miller. I would think the grocer's and Ironmonger's shop was down the side in Church Street as the front windows still look like offices. The shop to the extreme right was Edmond Nicholls a Baker 1888-1899.

West Street from a post card dated 1903. By this time Mr Hollyman, a saddler, who came to Butstone House in1894 had extended the Church Street shop into one side of Willett's offices on West street, you can see the sun blind over the shop window. In the mid 1930's Mr Hollyman moved to Sheldon's old Blacksmith's shop in Church Street opposite the Mill.

Although this postcard is post dated 1903. The photograph must have been taken earlier as the building on the right under the "Accommodation For Cyclists" sign is still a baker's shop. This was sold by Edmond Nicholl's widow Elizabeth in 1899 to baker William Byles who in turn sold the shop to Stuckey's Bank in 1902.

Top of West Street in 1894. The two ladies in black stand over the Butstone. The building behind them we knew as the Nat West bank is still Edmund Nicholl's bakery. It is a pity the railings to the left are not still there as it would stop people parking on this wide bit of pavement. The small stone wall that adjoined these railing was only taken down in the 1970s by Smarts who bought Clark's Electric shop No 10 West Street further down.

Walt Fisher outside his butcher's shop, No 8 West Street, just down from the Butstone in the 1930s. In 1919 the butcher here was Charles Stark whose delivery cart we see in the next picture. This shop has also been Hardwick's photographer's, Badman's Hairdressers, Semple's Fruiterer & Greengrocer and lately in this century Linda's Ladies Hairdressers. To the extreme left you can still see the dwarf wall, and extreme right, the remains of the railings I mentioned in the last picture.

Stark's butcher's cart, Stark later moved to The Square then to Axbridge.

To the right Badman's hairdressers, the same shop where Stark and Fisher had their butcher's business, next is Ella Clark's, the lady in the picture with her back to the shop. She sold all electrical goods and charged accumulators, early batteries for radios. A few yards further down the road by the telephone box, you can just see to the left of this picture, Mrs Clark's husband Ron and PC Basil Stockbridge were killed during the bombing of Banwell in September 1940.

In 1971 Chris Smart, a Weston newsagent, took over this shop before moving later to the present paper shop further down the road in 1977. Note the dwarf wall, mentioned before, between the two shops, the removal of which enables today's residents of these properties to park their cars here blocking the pavement.

To the left is Taylor's Stores and Post Office whose shop front seems to have changed three times between 1900 and 1940 according to photographs I have. German bombs destroyed this shop in September 1940 without killing any of the people inside. This shop, after being rebuilt, later became the Co-op.

Taylor's Central Stores as it was before it was bombed with Bill Knight, odd job man and driver, Ciss Yarde and Gladys Batten, shop assistants, Bill Rawlins, grocer and Andrew Williams, a driver, outside. After the bombing the Post Office was transferred, for a short time, to the Beehive Café, where Emery Gate is now.

The Top of West Street from just below the present War Memorial from a postcard dated 1909. Taylor's shop again to the right but looking as it did when owned by Peter John Wilkins, Draper & Grocer, 1889 to 1906 and called "Cheapside". To the left where the girl is standing was where one of the village pumps stood. This pump was paid for by a bequest in 1875 from William Tutt, a boot & shoe maker, and member of the United Methodist Free Churches Society whose Chapel was in Church Street. Much later Banwell's public telephone box stood near the same spot as Tutt's pump.

The house on the left, opposite Taylor's shop with a very low roof line, is so situated because, according to the Tuckey-Bennett map of 1770, a road or track descended here into the pond and came out again by the present butcher's shop.

The house with the gas lamp outside, No 14, has under its front yard two "cells", which I have been told, were for holding people before they were taken into custody in Axbridge Police Station. We believe this was the place that George Bennett refers to in his unpublished history of Banwell when he says, "a little below the Ship on the right side of the road lately has been erected a square building at the expense of £50 to the parish for a lock-up-house or prison for confining refractory and thievish chaps previous to their committal to legal prison, as to its proprietary usefulness we shall say nothing but as for look of it it is anything but ornamental to the Village". He continues "the ridiculous building above-mentioned was totally destroyed by a licentious mob on the 1st December 1830 occasioned by the indiscreet meddling of a certain person dressed in a little authority".

This riot seems to have happened when the local Constable Thomas Tripp locked up William Broadbear Jnr who had been fighting with a Thomas Dove. Broadbear was later released by two men named Watts & Stockman who broke open the lock-up door, all this with a great number of people assembled to cheer them on. Later, some of the Banwell men proceeded to take down the lock-up and go away with the materials. This caused a notice to be posted on December 7th about the "Riot and Felony" at Banwell and set a reward for the apprehension of those concerned. Ironically, this riot may have been fuelled by the fact that Broadbear's family lived behind the lock-up.

Below, Yatton's square lock-up, did Banwell's look like this, and if so I can see why George Bennett said "anything but ornamental to the village".

RIOT
AND
FELONY.

WHEREAS a Riotous and tumultuous Mob, assembled at BANWELL, on Tuesday, the 30th day of November last, and again on Wednesday, the 1st of December, and did then and there proceed to rescue a Prisoner confined in the LOCK UP HOUSE; and to pull down and set on Fire, the said Lock-up House: And whereas, David Watts, John Brown, George Stockham, Joseph Ureh, and James Broadbeard, have been severally apprehended and Committed to Ilchester Goal, for the said Offence.

And Whereas, Isaac Coleman, *Shoemaker*, Thomas Dove, *Butcher*, James Stephens, (alias Hou,) *Plasterer and Tiler*, Joseph Shallis, late a *Gentleman's Servant*, Samuel Knott, *Labourer*, Charles Hurley, *Mason*, James Fletcher, *Labourer*, William Fletcher, *Labourer*, Evan Brown, *Labourer*, William Broadbeard, *Mason*, and Thomas Davies, *Mason*, stand Charged with aiding and encouraging the said Riot and Felony, and have since absconded.

A REWARD

will be Paid by the Parish Officers of Banwell, over and above any Reward offered by the Government, for the Apprehension and Conviction of either, or all, of the above named Persons.

Apply to THOMAS TRIPP,
CONSTABLE

Dated Banwell, December the 7th, 1830.

C. GLANVILL, PRINTER, BOOKBINDER, &c. AXBRIDGE.

The deeds of this house, No 14, mentions the measurement of the frontage and says "which piece of land was formerly the site of the **round house** and public stocks but now paved over and enclosed with iron railings". George Bennett says the lock-up was square but, a round house, as most of them appear to be, is mentioned in the deeds.

Postcard dated 1912. To the left the Misses Hollier's Fancy Repository selling the goods you would find in a hardware store today. Their father, Mr William Hollier 1866-1923, was a plumber and painter & decorator at the same address. Later in the 1940s and 1950s Jack Neads, who sold all house furnishing, ran this shop. The next shop up where the lady is on the edge of the pavement was Alice Dibble a Dress and Mantle maker 1889-1910. Later Miss E E Bricknell. had a small draper's shop there.

*Another view of Hollier's
Fancy Repository*

Opposite Hollier's in the 1920's was John Edward Keate's pork butcher's shop, on the extreme right. John Keate at one time also lit the gaslights in the village and put them out in the morning, see Gas Works later. In this picture, taken in the 1950s, Keate's shop was run by John's widow, who was deaf and used an ear trumpet. She sold medlars, greengrocery and lemonade. This shop with the cottage next door was pulled down about 1968 to make way for the detached house that now stands out like a sore thumb. Further up the road on the right, was in the 1950s Banwell's telephone exchange and the rebuilt Taylor's bombed shop, now the Co-op, with a separate shop for the Post Office.

We complain today about advertising boards, but as you see from this photograph of Mr Clark's Boot and Cycle shop, it was worse long ago. The wooden structure above Mr Clark's shop where he repaired his boots and shoes always looked to me like something out of the Wild West. But it was stronger than it looked as the local council found out when they declared it unsafe in the 1990s following an accident in which a car ran into the shop and down into its cellar. The local council were called but instead of shoring up the building which would have interfered with the traffic flow, they persuaded the owner to agree to its being pulled down as being unsafe. This they succeeded in doing, but it took them a long time and plenty of cutting of timber before it finally gave way.

Byles' bakery to the right was previously a butcher's shop run by two generations of the Lawrence family. From 1891 till 1927 William Byles had this shop and I believe installed the bread ovens that were last used in 1994. These ovens have since been removed. At one time Mr Clark used the Byles' baker's shop on the opposite side of the road for selling his shoes and boots. Mr Byles had moved across the road to the Beehive where Emery Gate is now but still used the bread ovens here at the back of this shop. After Byles left in 1927 came Weeks, 1928, Lack, 1929, Abbott, 1975, Davison, 1982 until 1994 when the Bakery closed.

William Byles, the wandering baker of Banwell, who had at various times four baker's shops in West Street between The Square and the Malt House. Here he is seen at the rear of the Beehive with his daughter Ethel and second wife Marion.

The Lack family and staff who ran the Banwell bakery from 1929 to1975 beside their delivery vans.

From L-R Tom Lack Jnr, Ted Yarde?, Tom Lack Snr, Stanley Lack & Bill Edwards.

Brown's Cash Stores Banwell and Winscombe. I can date this photograph as the notice showing in the door advertising a concert at the Institute organised by the Fire Brigade is dated Friday 28th February 1908. This shop changed from a grocer's to a butcher's shop in the 1920s and is run today by the butcher Alan Vickery. Previous proprietors were Warboy drapers, Dunn grocers, Criddle, Newton, Neads and Stuckey butchers. The door to the right is now the door to the Post Office.

Banwell Pond from a Postcard dated 1909

Quite a different picture of the pond with it being cleared of mud that came up from the spring with the water. You can just see the swan on the far side where normally the depth of the water would be around 4 to 5 feet.

Although not that deep many have drowned in the pond including one of my Horle ancestors, Edward, son of James & Sarah aged three who drowned in 1826. Before that in 1767 Isaac Emery drowned in the mill tail.

In 1884 George Goding, John Duckett, Thomas Barrington and William Jacob Harris were indicted for the manslaughter of Richard Thomas. It seems Richard Thomas was drunk in the Square and had a fight with a man named Phillips. Someone suggested Thomas needed cooling off so after more fighting either Harris, Duckett, Goding or Barrington threw Richard Thomas in the pond on the Church Street side. Thomas managed to get to the island in the middle of the pond and sat there for some time; he then jumped or fell into the water and when recovered was dead. After the court case the jury took only ten minutes to acquit all those charged, the men seem to have been saved by the fact that Richard Thomas was alive, but drunk, on the island of the pond when he jumped of his own accord or fell into the water where he drowned.

To the left the Beehive about 1918-19 with William Byles the baker here

Before Byles' the Beehive was Irish, House & Co Drapers & Grocers. Next door was Miss Lucy Warboys a Draper. The house to the right of the Warboys that is now the Post Office belonged to Mr & Mrs Jack Raines whose kitchen or scullery was at a lower level around the corner where you can see today in the wall the shape of what looks like a church doorway.

Baker Byles' staff outside the Beehive circa 1918, Back Row, Not Known, Mark Byles, Ted Tucker, Henry Buncombe. Front Row, Sam Price, Bert Hewlett, Not Known, Jim Salter. The square floor tiles covered the whole area out to the pavement. A saying you used to hear about the village when Byles were bakers was "Billy Byles Baker Banwell Bakes Best Brown Bread", I am not sure if it was true!

In the 1950's the Beehive was a café run by Charles Broughton; later, after a couple of new owners the business closed. Around 1964 when the Beehive was derelict it was sold to the Co-op who at that time had a shop where Taylor's shop had been bombed opposite the War Memorial, now Coronette Coiffure & Clippers. The Co-op had a plan, in conjunction with Axbridge Rural District Council, to pull down the Beehive with two cottages next door and the shop (No's 30,32 & 34 West street), and build new "modern" shops there with car park, behind. Although the idea was good in that Banwell would get its much needed car park the thought of replacing these cottages with 1960s shops would not have improved the look of the street. After the Beehive was demolished in 1965 the Co-op put a temporary porta-cabin type shop on the site in 1968. This was not successful and it was removed in 1971.

The Bristol Co-operative Society's proposed development in West Street, Banwell. In addition to the shops and flats illustrated, the scheme also provides for a car park for 40 cars.

Artist's impression of the Co-op's proposed redevelopment that thankfully never happened

Lower part of West Street from a postcard dated 1905

To the left the Wesleyan Methodist Chapel built in 1862 presumably to replace the one in East Street that became the Literary Institute. To the right is what we knew in the 1950s as the Beehive Café, now the entrance into Emery Gate. In this picture it looks like Irish, House & Co Grocers & Drapers are still at the Beehive, circa 1902. Later Byles, whose bread delivery vans can be seen the other side of the road, took over the Beehive.

The house now No 30, known as "Stonehouse", next to the Beehive, is referred to in an 1846 mortgage "by the messuage know by the name of the Globe Inn" in the ownership of Richard Tuckey and before that according to the church rates it was called the "Hand and Pen". It seems that at this time No 32, next door, was part of the same house. This property was left to Thomas & George Wilcox masons in 1839 who split it into two premises. Thomas's part No 30 was "new built" which I think consisted of enhancing the frontage with door and window surrounds and raising the front wall to give a parapet.

The third building, the shop in this row, on the east side of Pruen's Lane, was where I believe Richard Tuckey's father, Joseph and brother, Edward had their stonemasons' yard in the late 18th century. The property is shown without a building fronting the road on Richard Tuckey's, 1770 map of the Town of Banwell.

From other photographs, other owners of this shop were William Bell Chemist & Veterinary Surgeon in 1894, and later in the 1930s Gulliver Grocers.

After the war this shop belonged to F P Day a grocer; when Mr Day died in 1972 and the shop was closed it was turned into two flats. The bottom flat was also used as a doctor's surgery for a period. During alterations of the shop Mr Welbourne, a local builder, found a large flat stone under the flagstone floor that can be described as a stonemason's practice piece. Amongst things carved on this stone was Joseph Tuckey's name with the date 1772 (see Search 14 page 51). This find may not confirm that this was where Tuckey's had their stonemasons' yard but I think it might help. Mr Welbourne put the date 1872 on the front face this restored building which I believe might be the date on which Tuckey's stonemasons' yard was first built.

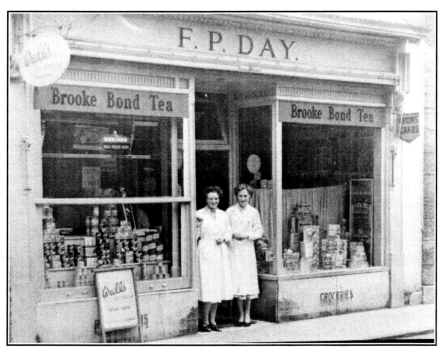

Possible site of Tuckey's Stonemasons' Yard circa 1760. The two local ladies in this picture are Barbara Buttimer, nee Newton and Kathleen Sweeting, nee Shankland.

To the left the reject tombstone or practice piece, at the top it reads, "Re thy creator in the days of thy youth 1772 Joseph Tuckey", and underneath is carved what looks like a skeleton figure and some odd words. To the right is a beautiful coat of arms carved by Edward Tuckey dated 1764 that can be seen in the bar of the The Bell Public House. Both Joseph Tuckey and his son Edward were landlords of the The Bell and Parish Clerks.

Richard Tuckey, Edward's brother, was also a schoolmaster and the person who produced the first good map of the "Town of Banwell" in 1770. Luckily George Bennett copied this map in 1812, as Tuckey's map no longer exists today.

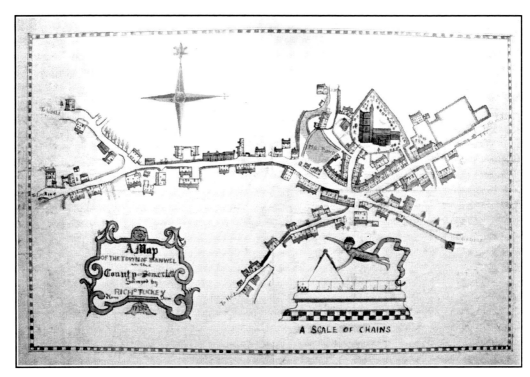

A copy of Richard Tuckey's map of the Town of Banwell 1770 drawn by Barry Pruen when a school boy

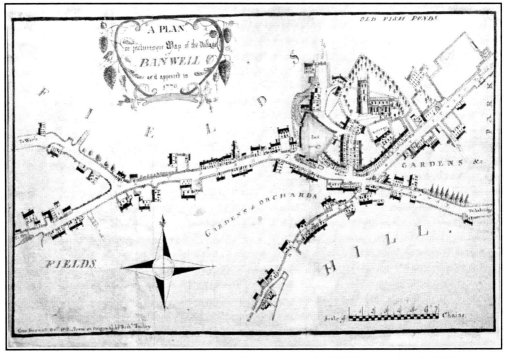

George Bennett's version of Richard Tuckey's 1770 map dated 1812

Lower part of West Street, the buildings to the right and behind the man in the road were destroyed by the German bombs in September 1940.

The interior of Greatorex's Shop, circa 1900-1912. Greatorex is listed as Chemist, Dentist and Wine & Spirits Merchant. He also published picture postcards of the village taken by photographer Fredrick Amos of Mendip Studios Banwell. From a shop invoice dated 1909 that he had sent to Miss Chapman of Stonebridge for her  "Girls Own" paper it seems that he must also have sold newspapers and books. I do not know if Mr Greatorex was a qualified dentist but I am told he drank a large tot of whiskey before starting on a patient and removed teeth without any form of anaesthetic. The shop was taken over by the Pruen family around the time of the First World War. The shop interior remained unaltered until the Pruens sold the paper shop to Smarts of Weston in the early 1970's. The shop is now Banwell News, our paper shop.

When I found this picture in amongst the family photographs of Virgo Neate (son of George Neate who had the two shops in The Square), I discarded it as not being in Banwell. It was not until I took note of the small dormer window above No 38 West Street, the Banwell Stores between the paper shop and library, that I realised that the picture was of Banwell. Looking through some billheads in the Banwell Society of Archaeology collection I came across one belonging to The London Drapery Company dated 1910, with proprietor Kinsey who later had a large draper's shop in Winscombe, now the Co-op. Perhaps the London Drapery Company was an early form of franchising.

In 1872 Henry Crook, shoemaker, had a business in Rodway (Castle Hill). He moved I believe to this shop in West Street in about 1889 until about 1902. He then went to a

shop on the corner of Church Street and the Church entrance. In 1919 a James Crook, bootmaker, appears in West Street. By 1927 the Church Street shop may have been closed, as there were then two Crooks, one a bootmaker and one a shoemaker listed in West Street until 1935. The same family were still here in the 1940's as Crook and Son Confectioners & Tobacconists. In the years after the Crooks left West Street for Church Street and before they came back Kinsey's (above) had their drapery there and in 1913 Herbert Pruen ran "The Banwell Creamery" here.

Although a poor picture, I have included it because of my interest in shop premises. James's Bakery, dated around 1902, is now the present library. I remember a Mr Fred James of the same family who was a farmer at Stonebridge and was often seen in the village wearing his brown leather gaiters. Before James's, a Mark Day, a postman, had a sweet and paper shop here. In 1913 our wandering baker, William Byles, was here.

Mrs Lewis outside her husband Samuel's tailor's shop with her nephew Ken Day, whose father ran the Builders & Undertakers business in The Square. Ken Day hit a saucepan of boiling water over his legs scalding them. He died shortly after, presumably of shock, aged 15 in 1924 and was given a Scouts Guard of Honour at his burial. The shop was across the Malt House entrance from the present library and was one of the casualties of the 1940 bombing in which Mr Lewis was killed. In Lewises' shop stood a grandfather clock made by John Coggings of Bridgwater that was also destroyed by the bombs except for the dial and part of the hands. Mr Windridge with whom Mr Lewis's son Percy lodged at one time gave me this clock dial, which I still have.

Mr William Woolfryes, the local solicitor, in his donkey cart outside three of the buildings destroyed by the bombs in 1940, now replaced by the "temporary", Public Toilets and two council flats Nos. 44 & 46. You can see Mr Lewis's tailor's shop behind the ladies in the picture. In the house to the left lived Edwin Thomas who with his brother ran a blacksmith shop in Church Street almost opposite the Brewers Arms. The Harris family occupied the house to the right of the Lewises' shop which ran down the lane to the Malt House where you can still see where their house was built into the Malt House's front wall.

In the picture the lady in the doorway is Mrs Thomas, the Child in the cart is Dolly Thomas, the boy on pavement is Arthur Thomas.

Mr Woolfryes is in the donkey cart and the ladies standing are Mrs Cotgrave, Mrs Turner and Mrs Woolfryes. The name of the lad stood with the donkey is Jack Raines.

Sadly, this is only a photocopy of a picture from a Banwell family's album now lost. This picture looks the other way to the previous one and shows the street scene that was lost by the bombing of 1940. From the right, first Lewis's, then Thomas's, both bombed, next No 48 (where brothers John, Wally and myself were born) and No 50; both these houses survived. The next two houses were also bombed, with the loss of two lives, but the one with the tall chimney was only partiality destroyed. This was rebuilt only to be demolished about 1968 to make the entrance to the car park.

42 to 54 West Street the morning after the bombing in September 1940

Fish & Chip Shop and Dynevor House 1947

According to George Bennett writing around 1812, "Mr Edward Wood has a good new house and a shop on the southern side of the street called West Street"; this was Dynevor House. At one time I thought that this shop might refer to the present fish and chip shop although it looks to have been built much later. Margaret Davis, whose family lived in Dynevor House from 1913 until it was demolished, wrote in Search No 8 page 24. "The shop part was a small sitting room with large window overlooking the horse mounting steps. The window was of one piece ¼ inch plate glass before the bombing in September 1940". Note the mounting block and last window to the west end of the house. On older photographs of these premises there were more buildings to the west end of the house that I believe were removed when the new school was built in 1926.

Dynevor House was destroyed in one weekend by a local builder in 1968. In the September of 1968 the Parish Council discussed the possibility of compulsorily purchasing the Dynevor House site for a car park and offering the earmarked car park site opposite the school to the developer in exchange. Sadly, these suggestions and others that would have made the situation outside the school far safer than it is today were never carried out. The site lay empty from that time until 1996 when School Close was built.

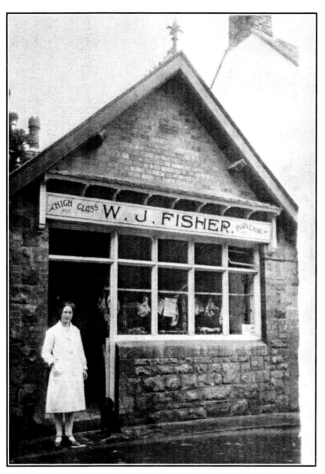

The Fish and Chip shop site has been used for that purpose since the Second World War; in the past this site or shop had been a tin maker's, a cooper's and as you see a butcher's. I have been told that this building was originally Fox & Fowlers Bank run by Ernest and Albert Davies.

Below is another photocopy from the now lost Banwell album. It shows Banwell Grange before the room over the front porch was removed, and shows again the cottages further up lost by the bombing in 1940. Two fluted columns that used to hold up a west gallery erected in Banwell Church in 1767 and taken down a hundred years later now support The Grange's porch.

The Grange where the Emery family, Mill owners, lived; the House was split into two parts during the 1950s. Behind The Grange in the 19th century was a tanyard. Here, possibly, the Emery family at leisure in The Grange – you may take off your coat but not your "top hat"!

Below. West Street nearly opposite Wolvershill corner. The building to the right had a stone relief above the windows on which was carved "Agricultural College"; it was possibly one of the early schools in the village. This building was mentioned in the Banwell Parish Council minutes of 1921, when it was left to the village and described as "formerly used as the Parish School and latterly know as The Stores was, by the Will of Sarah Ann Urch Gill deceased, bequeathed to the Banwell Parish Council for the purpose of a Public Hall".

By 1921 the west side of the building seems to have been converted, with an internal raised loading bay where, at one time, Mr Talbot, Landlord of The Ship kept a horse drawn wagonette. The parish bier, which still exists, was also kept on the left hand side of this loading bay. In 1922 after a parish meeting on the viability of using the old "Banwell Parochial School" as a Memorial Hall, the parish council of the day decided that it was not advisable to accept the gift and take over the building. The building was sold and it seems the money invested into what was to become "The Gill Charity". This charity's funds were eventually used with other funds to help pay for the present Village Hall in Westfield Road.

I am not sure of the building's date, but looking through a list of Banwell Schools compiled by the late Betty Tabrett there are two possibilities, one dated 1800 "a National School was provided for 100 pupils opposite the turning to Wolvershill road", or 1824 "A new National School was built on land given by the Bishop". This could be two different references to the same school. On the same list, dated in the 1890s, it gives Miss Mary Chapman of Stonebridge attended this school and the last teachers were a Miss Chapel and Miss Clark.

STICKY WALLACE

In the 1940s -1950s Mr "Sticky" Wallace, who ran a curio and second hand furniture shop, owned this old school building. Most of the village people getting married during this time bought their furniture from Mr Wallace. His nickname seems to come from a saying you do not hear much these days "sticks of furniture". Mr Wallace could always be seen on Fridays walking back from the paper shop studying the Weston Mercury's "For Sale" column through a spyglass and chewing a violet. This building was pulled down for road widening c1968.

Before being in West Street Mr Wallace had a shop in Church Street next to the pond and what might be called a Tinker's Cart. He used this in the summer to go around the country selling his wares. It is said he travelled from Land's End to John O'Groats twice with this cart. In the winter the cart would be left down Riverside at Creighton's Wagon Works.

Mrs "Sticky" Wallace with the "Tinker's Cart" on the road

Banwell House on the corner of West Street and Wolvershill Road, one time home of the Castle Brewery Family but remembered today as Dr Taylor's house. On the corner of the wall, behind the finger post directional sign, that is there now, is a piece of freestone on which was carved, "To Weston and Uphill", and, "To Worle & the Railway Station". These letters were chiselled away during the last war so as not to help the enemy if they invaded. The station referred to is "Puxton" station in St Georges.

On the corner of Whitecross Lane and Wolvershill Road in the 1930s. Bricknell's Sweet Shop on the extreme right behind the main house.

In the 1960s under different ownership this shop sold Government surplus stock.

Below. The Harris Family cottages to the right of Littlefield footpath. The horse drawn vehicles belong to Jacob Harris seen in the top hat. He also ran a coalman's business and supplied horses to pull the Banwell Fire Engine when needed. Two of the people at the doorway are Tom Harris and Annie Harris. The Building to the right of the parked cart is The Gables built for some of the Castle family.

Yarde's cottage jutting out into the road just before the turning to Westfield Road; it was hit by a bus in the 1950s and its east wall severely cracked. The cottage was deemed to be dangerous and was pulled down rather than repaired, this decision being possibly promoted by the district council who could see a way of widening the road here. You can still see the archway under the last cottage on West Street before Westfield Road.

Heathfield House, West Street, previously called "The Myrtles" when it was occupied by John Hungerford Powell in 1891. John H Powell was a local Solicitor who lived here prior to his marriage, when he moved to Elmhurst in Wolvershill Road where he later committed suicide before he could be arrested for embezzlement. Elmhurst is now two houses called Draycott Lodge and Golling.

Unfortunately, Heathfield House burnt down in 1956 and the present house, now called Mulberry Cottage, was raised on the ruins. In the early 1700's the house on this site was recorded as "Manor House and twelve acres—".

Heathfield House across the road from the bottom of Westfield Road circa 1891

The house in the background is Banwell Cottage

Two views of the same garage built by Mrs Day in 1919 and run by her son Francis until 1930. In the top picture is Reginald Yarde who, with his brothers, Fredrick, Edward and Ernest, ran the garage until 1934. After the Yardes came Clifford Mores, holding the door open below in this very cracked photograph. Mr Mores rebuilt the garage about 1955 and retired in 1959.

The New and the Old on the road, this is just past the Banwell Motors on Knightcott Road. This was the width of the road until the late 1950s when it was widened on the south side. Banwell Garage was at this time in the hands of the Yarde Family.

Francis Day, who ran Banwell garage before the Yarde Brothers, was an exceptionally gifted person in all trades. As a boy he made lead soldiers and sold them from his mother's house in the Rhoddy. He later made his own model airplane engines.

Francis Day's Lorry

L-R   Not known, Reginald Yarde, Francis Day, Hubert Day, Francis's father – known as Spider, c1920.

Another Banwell traffic jam, this time on Knightcott Road between Banwell Garage and The Whistling Duck before the road was widened in the late 1950s.

The Smiths Arms on Knightcott Road. The census for 1851 & 1861 lists Samuel Thomas a blacksmith at this property, whilst the 1871census lists Thomas Thomas as a blacksmith and innkeeper; perhaps this is how the Smiths Arms got its name. From 1872 to 1919 it was run first by George Stephens and later Alfred Stephens according to Kelly's Directories. The Smiths Arms eventually became Frank Curry's farmhouse. The house was later pulled down and in 1974 the Whistling Duck built in its place.

The south side of Baytree Farm from a postcard dated 1907. This house is usually seen from the north side and is now the offices of "Boulters Of Banwell".

George Bennett writing about 1812 mentions it belonged to the Keen Family and that he had in his possession a conveyance for Keene's estate at Knightcott dated November 6th 1506, that could probably date the house. Luckily the house still retains many of its original features even after being used as commercial premises for a number of years. Sadly a bay tree, though probably not the original, which grew at the north east corner of the property was removed in 2003.

Ernest Gait's garage at Knightcott in the 1930s

The main Banwell to Weston road at Knightcott in 1894. Looking towards Banwell, the cottage in the middle of the picture stands more or less where Knightcott Motors Garage is now. The new main road now goes the other side of this cottage. The road to the right will lead you to High Street and to the Caves. To the left of the man was

The Mitre that appears to have been built about 1851 with John Cheatham as innkeeper; by 1871 the same people were living there but no-one was listed as an innkeeper. Dennis Day's father told him a story that the landlord of The Mitre was not doing much business so he killed a rabbit and spread its blood over the old water pump in the wall of Bowman's Batch, opposite the above cottage. He then let it be known in the village that a murder had been committed at Knightcott. Whether the landlord got the increase in trade he wanted from those that came to see the scene of the crime I do not know, but he must have been found out in he end.

Well Lane at Knightcott leading up to the Caves and High Street in 1893. The cottage you can see in the distance belonging to the Caves estate has disappeared but was still partially standing in the 1950s. It was always referred to as "Jimmy Living's" cottage. The house to the left is called Roughmoor.

❑ ❑ ❑ ❑ ❑

The Rhoddy or Castle Hill

Bottom of the Rhoddy in 1893. The writing on the signboard to the left looks like Charles William George who is listed in Kelly's Directory for 1894 as a shoemaker.

Mr Jack Gardner's grocery and paper shop with his small bicycle repair workshop to the left. This shop was converted into a dwelling in about 1963.

Further up the Rhoddy looking down, the cottages are still there but the building in between has gone

Below.
Top of the Rhoddy in 1893 with Dark Lane still an unmade road. Dark Lane was called Back Lane on Richard Tuckey's 1770 Banwell map

Two views of the same cottage at the top of the Rhoddy, circa 1910

Top of Banwell Rhoddy or Castle Hill from a postcard dated 1950

Banwell Castle built as a home in 1847 by Joseph Dyer-Sympson who later restored the Abbey in the 1870s. The inner Courtyard and House c1880

The thatched cottage that was opposite the Castle, the home of the Sugg family around the time of the First World War. Sadly the cottage burned down and was not rebuilt as it was. Between the two cottages, looking like a ruin, was a very large glass hothouse in 1894.

The Gamekeeper's cottage in the middle of "Castle Woods". The last family to use this cottage, that had no water or well, were the Hunts. Jim Hunt, who was born here in 1913, said he took buckets down to Eastermead on the way to school and brought them back home full of water after school. The cottage when derelict was eventually pulled down when a "replacement" was built near to the woods' entrance.

The Hockey Field Cottage on Banwell Hill about one field east of the Caves wood. The cottage disappeared a long time ago but the area is still called the Hockey Field by some locals.

The picture here is about 1911.

Back row standing	Ron Clark, Edith Hurley, Mrs Fred James, Mrs Kerton, Miss Neate, Mrs Higginbottom, Mrs Bill Venn, Mrs Charlie Neate, Miss King, Elsie Clark, Grace Pruen.
Seated	Mrs Hawkins, Miss Elizabeth Shallish, Winnie Pruen, Mrs Powell, Mrs Castle, Miss Foll, Miss Hollier, Mrs F Day.
On the ground	Alba Tidball, Mrs Gyde, Mrs Winstone, Miss Hilda Clark, Mrs Gardner, Winnie Daw.

Stone on Banwell Hill east of the Caves wood erected by William Beard of Bone Cottage. Below is the text written on the stone.

A Human Skeleton Discovered near Bishops Cottage.
1842.
Beard with his kindness brought me to this spot
As one unknown and long forgot
He made my grave and buried me here
When there was no kind friend to shed a tear
My bones are here my spirit is fled
And for years unknown numbered with the dead
Reader as I am so shall you be
Prepare for death and follow me

Bishop Law's tower in the middle of the Caves wood built in 1840 as a folly, pictured here in 1893

❏ ❏ ❏ ❏ ❏

HARDING'S LANE now HIGH STREET

No one really knows why what we now call High Street was called Harding's Lane but it was so called on an estate map of Richard Taylor dated 1772 and led to one of his properties, an orchard with a building on it called "Harding's Barn". Was this how the lane got it's name?

A similar situation happened in West Street where locals call the lane that goes down the side of the paper shop to the field Ten Acres, "Pruen's Lane". For over fifty years the Pruen family owned the paper shop whose house, garages and stables ran down this lane.

The George public house in High Street looking very much as it is today but without the sign over the door, it closed about 1959. At the top of the hill you can just see the sign of the other public house in High Street – The White Hart usually called the "Top House"

My grandmother Laura Cruse in all her finery outside the The White Hart, or Top House, on High Street or as it was then called Harding's Lane. Laura's mother and father were landlords of this public house from 1906 to 1932; sadly, the photograph that comes from our family album was very much trimmed so we cannot see much of the front of the building.

Just before the Narrows in High Street where Rock Path and Hill Path lead onto Banwell Hill

John Horsington Grigg a writer of a manuscript, "Recollections of Banwell 1800-1861", now sadly lost. The Rev Samuel Taylor, Vicar of Banwell, copied many extracts from Grigg's recollections and published them in the Church Magazine in 1909. Grigg was also a Wood Artist; two examples of his work are shown in this picture of him. Banwell Society of Archaeology has one of his pictures depicting Banwell Mill. Grigg lived in High Street somewhere opposite Rainbow Cottage where I think this picture was taken.

The Narrows in High Street not much changed today. Behind the van, on the left hand side of the road, in the 1920s was Hemmin's pork butcher's shop. The shop was still open in the 1950s selling sweets.

High Street just after the Narrows; the cottage with garage attached on the left was partially demolished in the mid 1950's and the road widened. The Jubilee Pump is by the telephone pole.

High street looking west past the Narrows, the cottage on the right was demolished to make way for two dwellings in the mid 1950s. The long house to the left, now at the top of Littlefields Rise, was the Preacher's House or Wesleyan Manse. It is described as 'newly built' when purchased from Thomas Horsington in April 1824 by the "Banwell Wesleyan Preachers Residences Charity". In 1881 it was no longer required as a "new more commodious residence had recently been acquired in East Street".

A view of High Street from Hill Path dated 1909

High Street 1893, the picture taken from somewhere near where the council houses start on both sides of the road

❑   ❑   ❑   ❑   ❑

Church Street

To the left Butstone House with the girls standing outside Mr Hollyman's harness and saddlers shop. Mr Hollyman came to this shop about 1894, later he took over the premises of Sheldon's the Blacksmith in Church Street. Across Church Street in 1902 the bakery became Stuckey's Bank. The bank later became Parr's, The London County Westminster & Parr's, the Westminster then Nat-West when it closed in 1991.

James Hunt's Carpenter, Joiner & Undertaker's shop circa 1902-1919, part of Arden House; the workshop window by the garage was replaced about 1977.

The Free Methodists built the Chapel next door in 1872 and a schoolroom was added in 1898. Perhaps the Free Methodists were a breakaway group from the West Street Chapel, but by 1889 "Hope Chapel", as it was called when auctioned, was bought by a Mr Clark who said "I will retain the premises as a place of worship". This Baptist Chapel later became the Parish Church Hall. The cottage adjoining was used by Banwell Society of Archaeology as a museum in 1980 until the Church sold all the premises.

Top of Church Street showing Tom Vale's butcher's shop, 1888-1927. Mr Vale, known as "Tripey", was not a very pleasant person as I can tell, as he used to lash out at us kids with his walking stick when we passed him outside No 30 West street where he lived in retirement. The shop window to the left below the boy was where John Cook circa 1848 and George Brake circa 1855 had their Draper's, Grocer's and Ironmonger's. George Brake was also a corn and seed factor as was Thomas Willett who was here circa 1875. Above this shop window you can see the first floor loading bay where Willett's stored grain from the mill. Lower down to the right of the line of people was the rear entrance to The Bell where horses could be stabled; this entrance went through into East Street. Behind the line of people you can see Henry Crook's shoe shop, 1906-1935.

A better photograph showing Cook's, Brake's and Willett's shop. Above the shop Willett's had extra storage for the mill; you can see the loading bay door and winch for raising sacks of grain, top left. The shop window to the right was Hardwick's Photographic Studios in the 1940 and 50's. The doorway behind the motorbike is still there with its half millstone doorstep.

Top of Church Street west side.

An early picture of the Church taken probably pre 1884 but certainly pre 1890. You will notice that the clock face is set in a "wooden surround" and is the clock dial belonging to the old 18th century clock that was replaced by Miss Fazakerley's clock from Denbigh Castle in 1884. Banwell's old clock was past its best. Miss Fazakerley's clock was fitted with gas lit dials one to the east one to the west. Although the clock must have performed perfectly the people of the village asked Miss Fazakerley to take back her clock which she did. Her clock was then replaced by one bought by public subscription from Dell of Bristol; this clock tells the time in Banwell to this day. Why Miss Fazakerley's clock was rejected I do not know but I suspect it was because of those "modern" gas lit dials. When in 1885 the Dell

clock was installed the old wooden dial may have been put back, if so the new clock dial listed in the church warden accounts for 1890 was a skeleton clock dial that fitted across the third window opening on the tower until 1937. During the restoration and re-hanging of the bells in 1937 a new solid clock dial was fitted above this window as we see it today. Noting the style and position of the church clock dial is quite useful for dating views of the village showing the church tower. See Banwell Church Clock & Bells, Roy Rice 1984

Banwell Church.

A similar view to the last but about 1905; notice the 1890 skeleton clock dial. In the shop with the blind to the extreme left in 1906 was shoemaker Henry Crook; about 1935 the business was taken over by Thomas Hudd boot repairer then in the 1950's by the Tucker family selling boots & shoes. After the Tuckers, the shop was turned into a private dwelling.

The brass memorial to John Martock, physician to Oliver King, Bishop of Bath & Wells, now on the wall of the south aisle of Banwell Church. Oliver King, who is known for rebuilding Bath Abbey in the perpendicular style, died at his manor house (the Abbey) on the 29th August 1503, and Martock died at Banwell two days later the 31st August 1503 so the two men were probably lying dead in Banwell at the same time. Martock's brass is unusual, so I am told, as it has Martock's Almuce, that looks like a collar with two tails hanging down, in lead let into the brass. The only other Somerset memorial brass with lead inlay is in Wells Cathedral.

Banwell Church Interior Pre 1862

One of the earliest photographs I know of the interior of the church. If you look closely you will see there are wooden steps up to the pulpit; according to the Rev Taylor writing in the Banwell church magazine in 1905, "the present stone steps replaced the wooden ones about forty years ago". This could be during a large restoration of the church that took place in 1862. The original stone steps of the pulpit were removed during the incumbency of the Rev Blinman Gresley (1747-1773), see George Bennett's History.

You will also see that there is no organ at the east end of the north aisle. At this time the organ would have been on the south side of the west gallery under the tower. The organ moved to the end of the north aisle about 1899. The extra seating in the centre of the nave seems unusual with such a large church as Banwell but the extra seating might have been needed at this time as everybody was expected to be in church on Sundays. The Population around 1861 was 1,853.

A different view across the pond. The house to the left, now called Mill House, is listed as "The Swan" in 1706. The road in front of this house was a thoroughfare to Church Street until closed in 1816. The building to the right shows the Brewery with its chimney that was, until the 1850s, a paper mill. To the extreme right is the grist mill building.

The earliest record of Thomas Emery at Banwell Mills is a baptism entry "1712 September 8 Thomas son of Thomas and Mary Emery –of ye Mills". Thomas Emery senior carried on the business of a paper manufacture, miller, tanner, and brewer? up to his death in 1747. According to George Bennett the tannery was behind the Grange. Thomas Emery Senior may have been a brewer in 1747 but I believe the brewery at Banwell came in the 1850s when the paper mill closed.

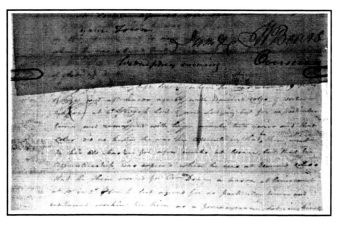

The 1837 Tithe Survey shows the Mill still belonging to the Emery family but run by Robert Alford & Company, (who also had a mill at Cheddar). In 1845 it was reported that the paper mill, which had been idle for several years past, was rented to George Pim paper manufacturer of Andover. The paper mill seems to have closed about 1850 when the Castle family took over the paper mill and started the brewery.

A piece of paper, (opposite, below), rescued by Wally Rice from the Axbridge Council Office concerning the examination of James Canterbury 28th day of January 1817 and signed by William Beard of the Bone Caves fame. Beard was Overseer to the poor at the time. The watermark on the paper is "BANWELL MILLS 1812". From records the Paper Mill was establish by 1710 at the latest.

1894

In front of the mill building, on what now looks like the lawn of the cottage, were the two water wheels; one small that went into the brewery and the other large that went into the mill building. My grandfather said he had never seen the small water wheel working, but I am told it drove a pump to take water to the top of the brewery building.

This model was made from memory by Jim Tabbrett of Winthill and was shown to various old Banwellians to confirm it was a good representation of the mill & brewery water wheels. The area where the water wheels stood is now the front lawn of Pond Cottage.

The large water wheel to the right kept turning until 1921 when Willets the Corn Merchants, who ran the mill from about 1870, moved to Sandford. Willets had their headquarters at Butstone House on the corner of West Street and Church Street where they once had an ironmonger's shop and used the upper stories for storage for the mill.

1894

Church Street or Mill Lane as it was sometimes called. The area between the steps and the girls with the pram is the cart-wash where there used to be a horse trough and tap put there to compensate the village for loosing its pond. There seems to be railings around the walkway to stop you falling into the water wheels but not into the pond.

Banwell Brewery is first listed as Thomas & John Castle in 1861, Thomas Castle in 1883, Castle & Rogers, in 1889 and Castle, Son and Wood in 1894. Many bottles and stone beer jars still exist from the brewery and the labels illustrated here show the extent of what they produced. The brewery closed around 1906. For the story of the Banwell Brewery See Search No 11 Page 9 by Betty Tabrett.

A sample of the brewery's products other than Beers and Stouts.

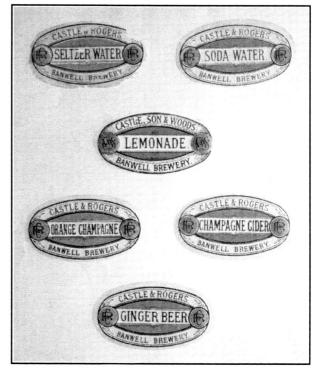

To the left is the mill building with the loading bay for taking in the grain on the first floor and below where the processed product came out. The men standing are Albert Brooks, Martin Denmead and Harry Merrick. The buildings behind the men belonged to the Brewery. On the opposite side of the road the first building on the right was Thomas Sheldon's blacksmith later Hollyman's a sadler and harness maker who left the business to his nephew Alfred Winstone. Next to Sheldon was another blacksmiths run by the Thomas brothers, one who was also landlord of the Brewers Arms. The shed behind the horse and cart on the far right was where Reg Thomas, son of one of the brothers, a wheelwright, repaired carts. Reg Thomas converted Farmer Gadd's 1920 Sunbeam car to carry the Merryweather Manual Fire Engine Miss Fazakerley had given the village in 1887. See Search 17, Banwell Fire Brigade.

Advert for Castle's Brewery it was later called Castle & Rogers, before becoming Castle Son & Wood

The opposite side of the road from the Brewery & Mill in 1939. The funeral procession of Fred Parker passing by Hollyman's, saddlers. Fred Day undertaker and builder of The Square is in the top hat with his son Dennis. Mr Parker who served in the Navy during the First World War was given a military funeral by members of the Fleet Air Arm who were stationed at Locking Camp. Fred Parker was also one of the men who helped knock down the brewery chimney in the 1920's, see Search 19.

A busy brewery yard dated 1897; the building to the left below the Brewery's chimney is the back of the bungalow cottage you pass on your way around the walkway from the butchers shop to the pond steps. The buildings to the right survived until the 1970's when they were pulled down. A new pump house is now on this spot.

A view from Ten Acres showing the back of the Brewery

The passing of Banwell's Pond

After the Brewery closed in 1906 it seems to have belonged to a Mr King who sold it, presumably with its water rights, to Bristol Water Works in 1909. They then sold it to Weston Urban District Council in 1914.

By an act of Parliament passed in August 1914 the Weston Urban District Council, as it was then, were able to take the spring water that had fed Banwell pond and worked the mills for centuries. This act, as you would expect, was fought against and even went to the House of Lords where in May 1914 Joseph Dibble of Plantation House put the case against the Bill for the village. As it happens, the Act was passed, but with a proviso that the pond might not be filled in or covered until "at or near the said pond a suitable and sufficient watering place for stock and for washing carts" was provided. The Council were to maintain and keep a supply of water there, and they should provide and maintain a stand pipe and that this stand pipe "shall be available for

use by the inhabitants of the village of Banwell for obtaining a supply of water for domestic purposes free of any cost." Also a supply of not less than five hundred thousand gallons of water to be put into Banwell River each day between June and October and two hundred and fifty thousand gallons between November and May.

The pond looking towards West Street as it might have looked between the mill closing and Weston Urban District Council filling in the pond.

In October 1922 a letter from Mr Brown, engineer and surveyor to Weston UDC, made suggestions as to the use of the area where the pond had been. He said "it is not practicable to restore the running water to the Pond" but gives various other suggestions which perhaps are worth consideration; amongst them were "water should be pumped into the pond" "and replenish it from time to time", "to level the surface and sow it with grass so it could be used as a bowling green", and "to lay out the space as an ornamental pleasure ground and plant it with shrubs".

In January 1923 Mr Brown's proposals were discussed and it was proposed, seconded and unanimously carried "that the Parish Council is of the opinion the desire of the majority of the inhabitants of Banwell to be that the pond be restored as nearly as possible to its original state". While all this was going on, Weston UDC had put a water tank at the site of the old pond for inhabitants to draw water, which was proving not to be very convenient. In March 1923 another meeting requested the WUDC "to make the bottom of the pond sufficiently sound to retain water and to refill the pond"; later at other meetings Banwell Parish Council were told by the Weston Urban District Council that sealing the base of the pond could not now be done and that they could not help with any cost other than levelling the pond area.

After much correspondence the pond area was turned into the third suggestion, an ornamental pleasure ground and what we know today as the "cart-wash" supplied. Not much of an exchange for the village pond!

Pond area with trees before becoming the bowling green in 1934

Lower part of Church Street in the mid 1960s; the building to the left was the Thomas Brothers blacksmiths' building intact with its forge still inside. Next up still on the left is what was Thomas Sheldon's blacksmith's shop but at this time Alfred Winston's saddlers and general ironmongery business.

Bottom of Church Street 1894. The cottage to the right is The Brewer's Arms. Prior to becoming a public house in 1861, people listed here were, 1815 John Nicholls, papermaker, 1822 Daniel Hemens, papermaker and family. By the 1851 census Daniel is described as "former papermaker" which is around the date we understand the paper mill closed. The first Landlord listed at The Brewers Arms is Thomas Parsley, Baker/Innkeeper 1861 followed by John A Thomas, Blacksmith/Innkeeper 1881, Charles Creighton, Beer-retailer 1892 and Samuel Spokes 1901.

Creighton's Wagon Works and saw pits, 1906-1935, that were owned for many years by Jim Emmerson. Access to the two doors on the first floor, this side of the building, where the carts were painted, was gained by a steep ramp made for the purpose.

Banwell river before the water was given away. The building to the left was one of the many slaughterhouses in the village; further up you can see the open timber sheds of Creighton's Wagon Works.

The field to the right of the river is know as "Ten Acres"; this field used to belong to the Brewery and was used for the Banwell Horse Show, as was the "Abbey Field" on the left behind Creighton's Wagon Works.

The Horse Show in Ten Acres in the early 1900s

NB. The tall house on the right was the malthouse for the brewery

The first Banwell Horse Show was held in 1880 at the suggestion of Loftus Ricketts who lived at what is now called The Elms in Wolvershill Road. The first show with Mr Ricketts as secretary was a success and the second year was even better with over 350 entries. It was decided to make it an annual event. Besides the usual competitions riding and jumping there was driving in single and double harness, tandem and four in hand and there were contests for shoeing for smiths and driving for ladies. Later, besides competitions for horse and ponies, there was the showing of cattle, sheep, pigs, poultry, butter and cheese with prizes for the best entry.

The Show in 1886 was held in "Ten Acres" and attracted nearly 600 entries; amongst the patrons were the Earls of Shrewsbury, Suffolk and Berkshire, so it was a very high profile event. The later events seem to be called Horse and "Agricultural" shows.

Horse Show in Abbey Field, 1898

*Horse Show in
Abbey Field
1898*

In 1887 the event, now under the secretaryship of Mr T Castle, was held at the Abbey Field by permission of Miss Fazakerley. Although entries were down by about 30 on the previous year, it was thought to have been brought about by the higher entrance fee and restricted area in the Abbey Field. It seems that sometimes the owner of the Abbey would put their ground at the disposal of the Horse Show and as these 1898 pictures show, it was sometimes held there so as not to cause offence.

Most important for the village was the build-up to the Horse Show, as all the entrances to the village had decorated arches across them and extra arches down West Street and the entrance to the show ground with flags adorning most houses. Some of the decorated arches had verses written on them such as "Success to the Show" or "May the Best Man Win". Dennis Day, whose father's building and undertaking business was in The Square, said his father's men took almost six weeks to build the large wooden grandstands and areas for the cattle, sheep and pigs. Seeing the size of these grandstands in the picture you can see why it took so long.

One of the many arches put up in the village for Banwell Horse Show this one outside Keate's and Hollier's in the narrow part of West Street just down from the War Memorial. There were other arches on all the roads leading into the village and many more like this one at various points in the streets.

Arch over the entrance to Pruen's lane opposite the Methodist Chapel. The arch here was for the end of the First World War but there was one here similar to this on Horse Show Day, as this was one of the entrances to Ten Acres where some of the Horse Shows were held.

In the 1920s the show became "The Banwell & Weston" as in some years it was held at Weston. Later it became The Banwell, Weston, Highbridge & Burnham Show. I have yet to find out when the show ceased, but it was still going in 1939 at Highbridge, 1949 at Hutton Moor, Weston and 1951 at R A F Station, Locking.

Banwell River from near the ash tree, not so big in this picture, about 1894. On the right the now ruined slaughterhouse, that burnt down in the 1960s. Note the gap in the river wall, where the man is standing, below which you can still see the stepping-stone although much mutilated by the mechanical river cleaners used in recent years.

Banwell Gas works extreme left and Upper Poorhouses adjoining. The cottages to the extreme right next to the Bow Bridge, now destroyed, contained yet another slaughterhouse used by Brafield's in The Square.

Banwell Gas and Coal Company was registered in November 1863 with local businessmen taking shares; by 1865 they had been joined by some of the gentry in the village. Besides supplying gas to street lights and some houses, the company supplied gas to the Church and was used to light Miss Fazakerley's clock dials on the church tower, before the clock she gave was removed in preference to the one bought by public subscription. Although the business started well and must have been that way for some time, I have been told that they were unable to keep up a good supply of gas and the business eventually failed. Percy Culling who bought the Gas Works in April 1919, put a "PS" to a letter he wrote to H Burke Esq. in May 1920: "during the last 12 months I have lost about £200 on these works." On the 15th December 1920 Percy Culling gave notice that he had been appointed Liquidator of the Banwell Gas and Coal Company, which does seem unusual, the owner being Liquidator.

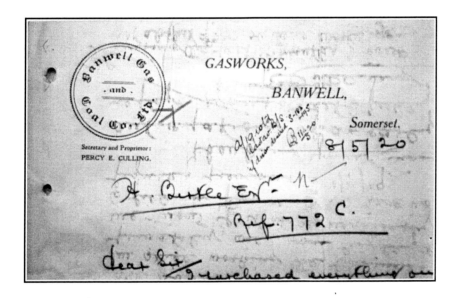

Bill Keate told me that his Uncle, John Keate, who had the pork butcher's shop in West Street at one time, lit the gaslights in the village and put them out in the morning. When the wind made it difficult to light the gas jets, John's young son Bert helped out by carrying the light pole while John carried the ladder to get closer to the gas jet. John was paid six shillings a week for sixteen lamps. There were gas lamps by the Fire Station, The Bell, at the entrance of the road into the Church, at the start of the pond (now Bowling Green) walkway in Church Street, opposite the pond steps in Church Street, and before Creighton's Wagon Works at Riverside. In West Street they were placed outside the Methodist Chapel, where the school is now, opposite The Grange and on Wolvershill Corner. In High Street, there was one by The White Hart, just before the Narrows and by the Preacher's House at the top of Littlefields Rise. There was one at the bottom of Dark Lane, and at the top and halfway down the Rhoddy.

The cottages to the right of the gas works were the Upper Poorhouse built in 1800 by James Caple of Winscombe; the Lower Poorhouse, no longer standing, went along the north side of th path on the entrance to Golling Lane.

In 1812 money was raised for these Poorhouses by the sale of the Wood House next to the pon and the Church House opposite the church entrance. After the Poor Union Law of 1834, the loca poor came under the jurisdiction of the Axbridge Union. The Upper Poorhouse came into th ownership of John Brake who sold the cottages to the Gas Company. See Somerset Industria Archaeology Society Bulletin 64 1993.

I always presumed that after 1834 all the people that would have gone to the local Poorhous went to the Union House, which for Banwell would have been the one at Axbridge. Nette Rice i her research has found that many of the families that might have been in the Poorhouse were sti there when John Brake owned the cottages. In 1851 10 people were there, in 1861 27 people. I 1871, now Brook Cottages and owned by the Banwell Gas Company, 51 people. I am not quit sure but it seems these people may have been the "second poor" who might have been able t support themselves to a certain extent; the "first poor" who had no chance of supportin themselves went to the Union House.

Sandford & Banwell station 1894. Although in Sandford parish I would think the station was built because of Banwell's size and industry rather than Sandford's. The line was built in 1870 and closed in 1965

❏   ❏   ❏   ❏   ❏

Part Two – Some People of Banwell

Banwell Church Bellringers 1976

Back   *Andrew Ogden, Colin Hornett, Steve Davies, Peter Everett, John Barrett, George Robson, Charles Eyre, Walter Rice.*
Middle   *Steve Robinson, Angela Bromwich, Sarah Rice, Alison Williams, Alison Hebden, Lynette Rice, Daisy Eyre.*
Front   *Roy Rice, David Bromwich, Reginald Dodson, Rev John Bromwich, Dr W A Taylor, Geoffrey Hebden, Michael Hebden.*

Banwell Bells 1937
Walter Day (bellringer), Fred Thorrell (bellhanger), Tom Cruse (bellringer), Fred Stephens (sexton),
Jack Shallish (bellringer),   Reverend Amos (Vicar).

Banwell Bells 1965

Wally Rice (bellringer), Walter Day (bellringer), Jack Elisbury (bellringer), John Irving Snr(local), Rev John Bromwich, Steve ------ (bellhanger), Richard Pruen (bellringer), Dawson's (steeplejack), John Irving (bellringer), Eric Fowler (bellhanger). Sitting in bells, Roy Rice (bellringer), Dennis Day (bellringer).

Banwell Bowling Club 1950s

BackRow   Mrs Venn, Reg Ingram, Charlie Parrott, Jack Cockerill, Arthur Kerton, Dennis day, Unknown, Mrs Badman, Unknown Mrs Reid.

Third   Charles Hunt, Mrs A Coombs, Unknown, Mr Llewellyn, Unknown, Unknown, Unknown, Clifford Coombs, Mr Ushe Mrs D Day.

Second   Unknown, Stanley Berry, Unkown, Bill Kerton, Unkown, Mrs H Kerton, Jack Neads, Gwen Mountain, Bill Venr

Front   Horald Pollard, Harry Kerton, Unkown, Mrs Picton Davies, Captain Picton Davies, Fred Millier, Fred Day Mrs H Pollard, Fred P Day.

Banwell Church Choir 1930

Back Row Harold Tidball, Charles Champney, Turp Hembury, Roy Hill, Leslie Harris, Reginald Harding, Edward King, Donald Warburton, Frank Shallish, Rolly Weeks, Douglas Gardner.

Third Mr Cray, Edward Lancaster, Jack Lukins, Walter Day, Nathaniel Day, Edgar Pope, Toby Hutchings, William Kerton.

Second Mr Batten, Harry Salter, Sunny Daw, Dr Anderson, Vicar Amos, Mr Walters, Joseph Price, Albert Salter, Dennis Day.

Front Percy Shallish, Herbert Palmer, Anthony Tisdale, Harold Harris, Hector Rains, Edward Buncombe, Robert Shallish, Raymond Daw.

Banwell Church Choir 1976

BackRow Walter Rice, Percy Baker, Michael Hebden, Steve Robinson, Geoffrey Everett, Peter Everett, Leonard Windridge, Arthur Elton-Clark, Geoffrey Hebden, Roy Rice.

Middle Reginald Dodson, Anette Williams, Caroline Durbin, Sharon Durbin, Claude Champion, Leonard Jones, Mrs Irving, Mrs Ivy Edwards, Mrs Winifred Rice, Gina Bridgeman, Dennis Day.

Front Andrew Bridgeman, George Mead, Preb A S Cran, Rev John Bromwich, Mrs Bromwich, Prof C Grunsel, Mark Buncombe.

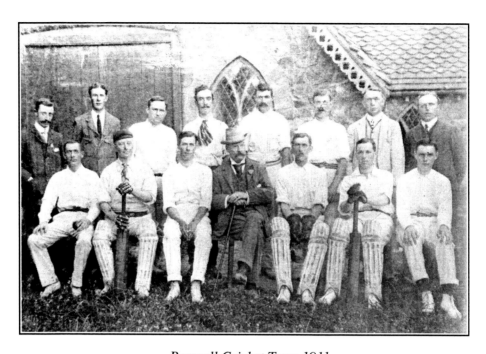

Banwell Cricket Team 1911

Back Row   L Serel, M Byles, S Norman, C Cruse, W Warburton, W Bright, FDay, H Tilley.
Front row   W Hunt, C Emery, C Hunt, Col A Richardson, J Lukins, E Troughton, T Castle.

Banwell Cricket Team 1930s

Back Row   Mr Alves, Mr Calvert, Walt Day, Jack Brafield, Charlie Hunt, Gerald Lukins, Bill Hunt.
Middle   Not Known, John Sheppard, Sunny Daw, Harry Salter, Reg Ingram.
Front   Eddie Merrick, Don Warburton.

Brewer's Arms Dart Team 1948
J Caffrey, F Adams, J Shankland, J Brafield, J Iverson, S Berry, P Caffery.
H Newton, Mrs Weekes Landlady, S Weekes, F Adams Jnr.

Banwell Firemen Circa 1908

Back Row   J Thomas, G Goding, O Day, T Hurley, W Pool.
Middle   F Small, H Crook, W Hollier.
Front   T Castle Captain, Mr Wickham secretary, F Say Lieutenant, Dr Caunter.

Six a Side Tournament 1938
Walter Harris, Jim Harris, Ken Sugg, Frank Fisher.
Sid Vale, Fred Parker, Bert Palmer.

Banwell Football Team 1920-21

Back Row   W Brown, S Parsons, F Sugg, T Harris, J Westlake, J Ellis, R Yarde.
Seated on Chairs   J Merrick, F Rook, B Salter.
Seated on Grass   G West, J Beans, B Keates, W Harris.

BANWELL FOOTBALL CLUB 1933-34

Back Row   J Ellis, E Merrick, A Maine, S Langford, J Harris, W Harris trainer, J Harris, A Neads.
Middle   H Leaves, J Avery, R Kinchin Vice Capt, R Calvert President, W Ellis Capt, W Neath, J Badman.
Front   B Robshaw, E Merrick, L Harris Hon Sec, A Westlake.

BANWELL FOOTBALL CLUB 1948-49

Standing L-R   E Fear, S Harris, J Harris, R Adams, R Saint, S Stenner, P Caffery, C Weeks, J Higgins, J Harris, T Harris.
Seated   G Warburton, V Larkin, G Harris, J Jones, R Thomas, B Harris, S Hewlett, H Thomas, H Harding.
On grass   A Crook, W Crook, G Hardwick, D Adams.

Banwell Guides & Brownies – 1950s

1 Marjory Harris, 2 Eva Hudd, 3 Janet Pollard, 4 Mary Parsons, 5 Mrs Stabler, 6 Anne Tabrett, 7 Anne Mores,
8 Mrs Harris, 9 Mrs Dawson, 10 Joan Ellis, 11 Esme Venn, 12 Mary Tabrett, 13 Wendy Leashman, 14 Joan White,
15 June Rice 16 Pam Smith, 17 Dorothy Newton, 18 Shirley Whitehead, 19 Shirley Smith, 20 Rosemary Sugg,
21 Miss Clark, 22 Annette Stanley, 23 Mary Gait, 24 Margaret Parsons, 25 Shirley Fletcher, 26 Pam Lear,
27 Gillian Durston, 28 Megan Morris, 29 Anne Osbaldeston, 30 Priscilla Mores, 31 Edna Loveridge, 32 Olive Carr,
33 Mary Loveridge, 34 Ishbell Dougherty, 35 Isabel Pruen, 36 Drena Steer, 37 Nancy Cousins, 38 Jean Carr,
39 Marina Welbourne

Possible Harvest Home Committee Pre 1914

Standing   *Thomas Cruse, Not Known, Herbert Castle, Not Known, Edwin Thomas, Mr Ham, not known, Nat Day, not known, Joseph Price, Edward Thomas, Alfred Harding, Mr A Hollyman, Samuel Lewis.*

Seated   *Charles Emery, Mr Glanville, Mrs Glanville, Rev Samuel Taylor, Dr Anderson, Joseph Dibble.*

Harvest Home Tea Ladies circa 1950s

L-R   *Mrs L Day, Miss E Buncombe, Miss M Creighton, Mrs Lukins, Mrs Gerret, Not Known, Mrs Byles, Mrs M Davis, Miss S Edwards, Mrs Hudd, Miss Sheppard, Mrs Irvin, Mrs I Edwards, Not Known, Mrs Parsons, Not Known, Mrs V Neate.*

Banwell Hockey Team 1929-30

Standing   B Pruen, M Seymore, T Parfitt, A Middleton, J Baker, Pillion.
Seated   K Vincent, A Coombs, M Hardwick, F Gyde, R Day, N Day, C Coombs

Banwell Hockey Team 1936-39

Standing   Reg Day, Raymond Lukins, Unknown, Unknown, Queenie Quick, Ivor Quick, Graham Hardwick.
Seated   Mike Hardwick, Unknown, Gerald Lukins, Edith Coombs and Ken Bird.

Helpers of the 1935 Jubilee tea for the Old Folks of Banwell at the Beehive

Standing   Mrs Mary Rains, Mrs V White, Mrs Salter, Mrs Merrick, Mrs Stevens, Mrs Cook, Clifford Cook, Mrs Brown, William Daw, Mrs W Rains, Mrs Batten, Mrs Byles.

Seated   Mrs R Thomas, Mrs S Harris, Mrs Ted Thomas, Mrs A Coombs, Mrs Venn, Mrs Lewis, Mrs Creighton, Miss Foll, Mrs Shallish

Banwell School 1953

Back Row   Brian Baker, Tim Rains, Brian Jones, Raymond Newton, David Warren, Tudor Neads, Norman Loveridge, John Harris, Graham King, Norman Evans, Robert McHardy, Miss Kennett.

Middle   Nancy Pruen, Pauline Horler, Peter Holmes, Gordon Rutt, Brian Horler, Nigel Holland, Simon Dougherty, Graham Griffin, Tony Hawkins, Robert Fletcher, John Davies, Susam Merrick, Carol Rains.

Front   Roy Rice, Christine Kenna, Susan Dougherty, Margaret Aplin, Mary Ambery, Angela Skidmore, Julie Broughton, Ann Scott, Wendy Lock, Richard Wall.

Out of this class of 34 only Myself Roy Rice and Richard Wall remain in the village.

MOTHERS UNION PHOTOGRAPH

Back row raised. 1or 2 Mrs Harry Lancaster. 3 Mrs Fred Day. 4 Mrs Champeny. 5 Mrs Venn. 7 Mrs Gulliver. 8 Mrs Coombs. 9 Mrs Byles. 10 Mrs Stevens. 11 Mrs Cruse. 12 Mrs Merrick. 13 Mrs Mark Day. 14 Mrs Leslie Day. 15 ?. 16 Mrs Ella Clark. 17 ?. 18 Mrs Nuttycombe. 19 Mrs Knight. 20 Mrs Lear.

Second standing 1 ?. 2 Mrs Shepbers?? Stephens?. 3 Mrs Quick. 4 Mrs Buncombe Ernie's 2nd wife? 5 Mrs Steel. 6 ? 7 ?. 8 Mrs Violet White. 9 Mrs Evan Merrick. 10 Mrs Jacob Harris. 11 ?. 12 Mrs Hunt Vera Merrick.? 13 Mrs Pollard. 14 Mrs Hinton. 15 ? . 16 Mrs Buncombe. 17 Mrs Harding (Sarah). 18 Mrs Mark Byles. 19 Mrs Gadd. 20 Mrs Lukins. 21 Mrs Hobbs. 22 ?.

Third seated 1 Mrs Quick Snr. 2 Mrs Dibble. 3 Mrs Batten. 4 Mrs Fred Harding. 5 Mrs Mary Rains. 6 Mrs Salter. 7 Mrs Creighton. 8 Mrs Foll. 9 Miss Osmond. 10 ?. 11 Mrs Ted Thomas. 12 Mrs Raines Kath's mother. 13 Mrs Millard. 14 Mrs Jack Gardiner. 15 Mrs Shallish. 16 Mrs Searle. 17 Mrs Joe Davis. 19 Mrs Hunt (Mary & Jims Mother). 19 Mrs Holluman.

Banwell Scouts 1925

Standing,   H Pruen Scoutmaster, Arnold Raines, Jack Neads, Victor Appleby, Barry Pruen, Ginger Harris, Bert Keates, Andrew Williams, Pete Fry, Mrs H Pruen Scoutmistress, Harry Marshall.

Seated   Jim Harris, Raymond Harris, Not Known, Cecil Tozer, Ivor Shallish.

On Grass   Reg Shallish, Jack Shallish, Jack Stock, Ginger Nuttycombe.

Banwell Scouts & Cubs 1949

Reginald Pollard, Wally Rice, John Rice, Tony Johnson, Bill Venn, Russell Rawlings, Bill Sanders, Colin Tabrett.

John Baker, Roger Black, Hubert Skidmore, Peter Charman, Kenneth Kenna, Brian King, Stanley Berry, John Baxter, Gordon Warburton.

Anthony Adams, Colin King, Mr De Andrade, Mr Cousins, Sally Johnson, Rev John Bromwich, Mr Sanderson, Ian Black, Graham Ellis.

Michael King, Nicky Tabbrett, Peter Gordon, John Hudd, Billy Osbaldeston.

Ship Hotel Skittles Team 1937-38

Back Row	W Edwards, H Batten, L Hucker, T Bailey.
Third	J Avery, E Trevor, F Day, W Ellis, F Larder, A Appleby.
Second	F Rook, D Warburton, B Day, R Hill, G Lukins, G Nuttycombe.
Front	E Merrick, H Filer.

Ship Hotel Skittles Team circa 1955

Back row	Tom Weaver, Ted King, Roy Hill.
Second	Den Day, Don Rains, Ginger Nuttycombe, Tom Bailey, Cecil Reid, Fred White, Jack Ellis, Wilfred Sugg.
Front	Dewy Davis, Jim Griffin, Bern Day, Jack Brafield, Don Warburton, Clifford Cook.

Banwell Church Sunday School 1947

Back Row   *Anthony Adams, Colin Tabbrett, Colin King, Sally Johnson, Joan Betts, Eva Hudd, Wally Rice John Rice, Colin Stabbins.*

Middle   *Priscilla Mores, Margaret Parsons, Brian Bishop, Mick Yarde, David Yarde, Jennifer Edwards, Shirley Fletcher, Mary Tabrett.*

Seated   *Bill Venn, Pam Lear, Mrs J Fletcher, Miss C Yarde, Mrs Dawson, Rev Dawson, Mrs Hunt, Martha Wright, Tony Johnson, Mary Parsons.*

Seated   *Bob Fletcher, Michael King, Michael Fletcher, ———Loveridge, Raymond Loveridge, Carol Rains, Anne Ford, John Davis, ————, ————, John Hudd.*

Banwell Tennis Club

Stan lack, Reg day, Mary Croker, ————, Marjory Winstone, Mabel Creighton, Betty Daw, Don Criddle, Raymond Daw. Bert Palmer, ————,————, Miss Cosgrave, ————, Hector Rains, Arthur Kerton.

Banwell Weight Lifting Club 1936

Back Row   Stan Lack, Roland Weeks, Hubert Skidmore, Jack Merrick, Ron Davis, Fred Travalton, Sid Hewlett.
Middle   Ken Venn, Charles Williams, Harold Harris, Roy Atkins, John Nuttycombe, Jim Hewlett.
Front   Ken Denmead, Bob Harris.

Banwell Tug of War Team 1952

Back Row   Norman Stephens, George Starkes, Clifford Thomas, Ron Ball, Ken Body.
Front Row   Ken Harding, Bob Harris, Ron Loud, John Clarke, Jim Starkes.

Members of Banwell's Thomas De Beckington Lodge No 3320
Royal Antediluvian Order of Buffaloes circa 1925.

Back Row   Mr Denmead, H Leaves, Jack Ellis, Not Known, Not Known, Not Known, Not Known.
Middle row   Not Known, William Salter, Not Known, Joseph Merrick, Not Known, Robert Yarde, Jack Williams, Gilbert Skidmore, Mr Sheppard, Alfred Winston.
Front Row   Jack Raines, Evan Merrick, Ernest Wilks, Not Known, Wilfred Raines, Not Known.
Lying down   Sidney Skeates.

Banwell Black & White Minstrels circa 1932

Back Row   Bill Stone, Walt Harris, Donald Criddle, Jake Harris, Mr Raines.
Middle Row   Mr Fearer, Vera Lancaster, Evelyn Criddle, Mrs Payne, Vera Loveridge, Jack Raines.
Front Row   Sam Wooley, Margery Grant, Jean Hill, Ron Pitcherd, Sheila Edwards, Kath Ingram, Mr Carmichael.

Banwell Men's Coach Outing – 1920s

1, Joe Shallish, 2, Jack Shallish, 3, Ted Shallish, 4, Bill Sugg,
5, Len Shallish, 6, Not Known, 7, Jack Ellis, 8, Fred Sugg,
9, Charlie Sugg, 10, Bill Buncombe, 11, Not Known,
12, Ralph Stabbins, 13, Tommy York, 14, Fred Rook,
15, Jack Merrick, 16, Bert Appleby, 17, Bill Keate, 18, Ted Fear,
9, Charlie Fletcher, 20, Dennis Cuff, 21 Vivian Small,
22, Joe Harding, 23, Charlie Stone, 24, Ted Harris,
25, Jake Harris, 26, Bert Palmer, 27, driver, 28, Charlie Ingram,
29, Bill Ingram, 30 Chris Merrick.

Banwell British legion Relay Team, 1926-27

L-R: Unknown, ,Jacob Harris, Arthur Neads, Bill Ellis

Coronation 1953 High Street

Mrs Venn, 2 Fred Parker, 3 Mr Venn, 4 Travarton 5 Charlie Williams, 6 Claude Champion, 7 Mrs Hawkins?, 8 Nurse Thomas, 9 Bill Venn, 10 Mrs Blackmore, 11 Mr Blackmore, 12 Mrs Shallish, 13 Williams, 14 Mrs Williams, 15 Mrs Harper, 16 Not Known 17 Mrs Champion, 18 Mrs Charman, 19 Mr Charman, 20 Mrs Heal, 21 Mr Harpen, 22 Douglas Gardner, 23 Mrs Gardner. 24 not Known, 25 Len Shallish, 26 Mrs Travarton 27 Ted Lancaster, 28 Mrs Landcaster, 29 Not Known, 30 Mrs Curl, 31 Amy Cruse, 32 Mrs Price 33 Douglas Hayward 34 Keith Griffeths, 35 Mrs Griffiths, 36 Mr Cunnack 37 Mrs Cunnack 38 Rose Hayward 39 Mrs Merrick 40 Mr Price 41 Eddie Cruse, 42 Jeffrey Hayward 43 Yvonne Griffiths 4 Mrs Grey, 45 Not Known 46 Roger Champion, 47 ? 48 Not Known 49 ? 50 Josie Harper, 51Josie Charman 52 Not Known, 3 George Harris, 54 Sally Bryant, 55 Not Known, 56 Kenney Bryant, 57 David Westlake, 58 Harper, 59 Maureen Fieldhouse,) Andy Ball, 61 Miss Ball, 62 Christopher Field, 63 John Field, 64 Graham Ellis, 65 Richard Gardner, 66 Rosemary Gardner, 67 Jean Price 68 Mrs Ball,, 69 Pauline Travarton, 71 Nigel Parker, 72 Brian King.

Coronation 1953 Riverside

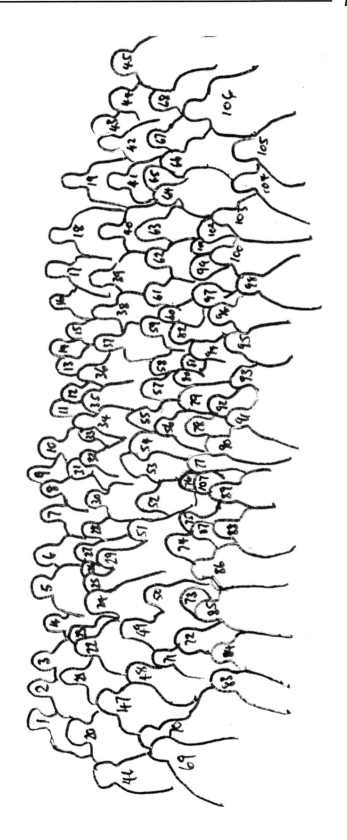

1 Merrick, 2 Shankland, 3 Mrs Shankland, 4 Mrs Corkwell, 5 Joe Merrick, 6 Dia Davies, 7 Charlie Pring, 8 Don Carr, 9 Ronnie Rains, 10 Mrs Rains, 11 Mr Gould,
12 Mrs Edie Coombs, 13 Janet Pring, 14 Mrs H Pring, 15 John Mc Hardy, 16 Jack Adams, 17 Rodney Pring, 18 Douglas Gould, 19 Tony Gould, 20 Mrs Wooly, 21 C C Corkwell,
22 Albert Clark, 23 Mrs Stabbins, 24 Ann Pring, 25 Myrtle Carpenter, 26 Mrs H Harris, 27 Victoria Harris, 28 Albert Adams, 29 Mrs Carpenter, 30 Mrs Gould,
31 Michael Clark, 32 Raymond Loveridge, 33 Not Known?, 34 Robert Mc Hardy?, 35 Mavis Loveridge, 36 Denise Weeks 37 Tessa Clark, 38 Sidney Pring, 39 Mrs Clark,
40 Peter Cardy, 41 Clifford Coombs, 42 Mrs Higgins, 43 Oliver Hornett, 44 Mildred Pring, 45 Mrs Davis, 46 Mrs Merrick, 47 Mrs Nuttycombe, 48 Grace Buncombe,
49Mrs Smith, 50 Jakie Smith, 51 Valerie Lumber, 52 Wendy Pring, 53 Loveridge, 54 Marina Welbourne, 55 Anne Harding, 56 John Harding, 57 Not Known?,
58 Winnie McHardy, 59 Shelia Cardy, 60 Sandra Cardy, 61 Ruby Clark, 62 Mrs Scott, 63 Mrs Adams, 64 Violet Carpenter, 65 Mrs D Appleby, 66 Mrs Newton, 67 Mrs Hornett,
68 Mrs Holland, 69 Bill Holland, 70 Mrs Joe Merrick, 71 Sandra Buncombe, 72 Joan Mc Hardy, 73 Cilia Smith, 74 Elinor Smith, 75 Shirley Smith, 76 Trevor Davies,
77 Jimmy Gould, 78 Norman Loveridge, 79 Joan Mc Hardy, 80 Carol Raines, 81 not Known?, 82 Valerie Adams, 83 Kenny Loveridge, 84 John Pring, 85 Pauline Sugg,
86 Anglia Adams, 87 ?, 88 Melvin Pring, 89 Peter Sugg, 90 Not Known?, 91 Nigel Holland, 92 Colin Hornett, 93 Not Known?, 94 Tommy Ellis, 95 Anne Scott,
96 Richard Harding, 97 Not Known?, 98 David Weeks, 99 Jean Carr, 100 Peter Venn, 101 June Smith, 102 Miss Smith, 103 Derek Newton, 104 Tony Adams,
105 Bert Adams, 106 Hector Newton, 107 Steve Harris.

Coronation 1953 Queens Road, Westfield

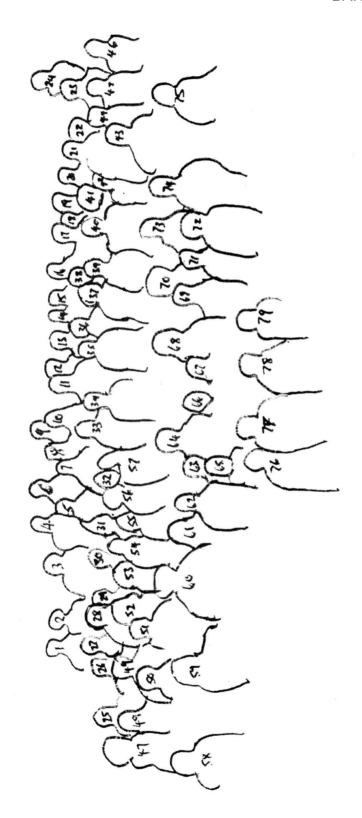

1 Cyntjia Aplin, 2 Anne Hull, 3 Rose Brooks, 4 Victor Larkin, 5 Ron Thomas, 6 Harold Sugg, 7 Jimmy Griffin, 8 Rex Ford, 9 Jack Baker, 10 Alf Smith, 11 Herbert Kenna, 12 Gladys Urch, 13 Mrs King, 14 Herbert Fear, 15 Brenda Price, 16 Les Price, 17 Fred Iverson, 18 Ray Harris, 19 Not Known?, 20 Not Known?, 21 Christine Kenna, 22 Mrs Davis, 23 Davis? 24 Davis?, 25 Ron Crook, 26 Not Known?, 27 Graham Warburton, 28 Elizabeth Price?, 29 Carol Hull, 30 Barbara Aplin, 31 Anne Ford, 32 Gordon Rutt, 33 John Kenna, 34 Melvin Brooks, 35 John Kenna 36 Mrs Kenna, 37 Mrs Phoebe Fear, 38 Mrs Price, 39 Fear, 40 Mrs Iverson, 41 Mrs Small, 42 Sylvia Small, 43 Trevor Iverson, 44 Not Known?, 45 Not Known?, 46 Tony Price, 47 Brenda Price, 48 Mrs Warburton, 49 Maj Smith, 50 Ford, 51 Sandra Ford, 52 Mrs Ford, 53 Mrs Ling, 54 Not Known?, 55 Not Known?, 56Not Known?, 57 Not Known?, 58 Graham Griffin, 59 Barbara Davis, 60 Mrs Jones, 61 Pat Davies, 62 Gordon Warburton, 63 Dave Ruby, 64 Eunice Ruby?, 65Not Known ?, 66 David Badman, 67 Not Known?, 68 Mrs Badman, 69 Kevin Sugg, 70 Mrs Sugg, 71Not Known, 72 Graham Griffin, 73 Brian Horler, 74 Brian Jones, 75 Not Known ?, 76 Jimmy Hewlett?, 77 Jackie Hewlett, 78 Brian Baker, 79 Roy Griffin.

Coronation 1953 Wolvershill & Knightcott

*1 Colin Stabbins, 2 Francis Claridge, 3 Gillian Mores, 4 Mrs Mores, 5 Margaret Osmond, 6 Mrs Quick, 7 Not Known
8 Not Known?, 9 Not Known?, 10 John Ellis, 11 Kathleen Claridge, 12 Mrs Counsell, 13 Marjory Grant,
14 Mrs Whitehead, 15 Mrs R Fear, 16 June Ellis, 17 Stanley Berry, 18 Silvia Eady, 19 Not Known?, 20 Mureen Eady
21 Not Known?, 22 Rose Ball, 23 Richard Wall, 24 Alan Jakeway, 25 Not Known?, 26 Not Known?, 27 Mary Ambery
28 Not Known?, 29 Roger Ellis, 30 Not Known?, 31 Not Known?, 32 Beryl Jakeway, 33 Maureen Wall, 34 Pat Wall,
35 Not Known?, 36 Not Known?, 37 Not Known?, 38 Susan Walker, 39 Tony Walker, 40 Not Known?,
41 Champany?, 42 Not Known?, 43 Not Known ?, 44 Sonia Connelly, 45Not Known?, 46 Margaret Quick,
47 Precilla Mores, 48 Larch Garard, 49 Alister Parker, 50 Rosemarie Stabler, 51 Mrs Champney?*

Coronation 1953 West Street

Back Row   1 Richard Pruen, 2 Bill Osbaldeston, 3 Diana Howells, 4 Anthony Adams, 5 John Hudd 6 Wally Rice,
7 Marilyn Newton, 8 Isabel Pruen, 9 Elizabeth Pruen, 10 Joyce Morgan, 11 Not Known, 12 Tony Yarde.
Middle   13 Roy Rice 14 Malcolm Criddle, 15 Tudor Neads, 16 Shelia Hebden, 17 Raymond Newton, 18 Nancy Pruen,
19 Veronica Adams, 20 David Pruen 21 Geoffrey Hebden
Front   22 Tony Hawkins, 23 Paul Mitchamore, 24 Josie Steer, 25 Mary Neads, 26 Josie Keate, 27 Pat Broughton
27 Not Known, 29 Susan Wall, 30 Michael Hebden, 31 Not Known, 32 Robert Pruen, 33 Not Known,
34 Not Known, 35 Caroline Lukins, 36Not Known, 37 David Criddle.

Coronation 1953 Castle Hill & Winthill

1 Ernest Kidner, 2 Maurice Bull, 3 Harry Stephens, 4 June Parsley, 5 George Parsley, 6 Jim Starkes, 7 Mr Larder, 8 George Starkes, 9 Mr Staddord, 10 Miss Bunty Calvert, 11 Mrs Ivy Bull nee Diamond, 12 Nellie Diamond, 13 Lillian Starkes 14 Mr Smith, 15 Mrs Lear, 16 Pam Lear, 17 Mrs Stephens, 18 Bessie Appleby, 19 Mrs Calvert, 20 Mrs Larder, 21 Mrs Edith Smith, 22 Mrs Gardiner, 23 Ethel Starkes, 24 Mrs Baker, 25 Stan Small, 26 Molly Nichols, 27 Mr Small, 28 Jim Nichols, 29 Mr Strong, 30 George Neads, 31 Beatrice Dowding, 32 Mrs Hawkins, 33 Mrs Strong, 34 Stuart Strong, 35 Jack Gardiner 36 Muriel Davies, 37 Dewey Davies, 38 George Dowding, 39 Bob Harris, 40 Jean Harris, 41 Sue Harris, 42 Mrs Harding, 43 Mrs Tripp, 44 Richard Baker, 45 Ken Baker, 46 John Davies, 47 Michael Davies, 48 Andrew Nichols, 49 Annette Dowding, 50 Marilyn Dowding.